MILLIONS OF AMERICANS'

JOBS
RAPED

BY AMERICA'S SO-CALLED "LEADERS"!

WE MUST STOP THEM!

By Peter Minnock-Stewart

Foreword by Jane Waterhouse

ISBN: 978-0-615-45409-2

Published by
M.E.C. Dougherty and Company
P.O. Box 7216
Wilton, Ct 06897

Manufactured in the United States of America

Cover design by Jack Disbrow

Book design by Celine Allen

Dedicated to
whoever is next…
a friend?
a neighbor?
We must stop the plunder!
We can! We must!

CONTENTS

A Note to the Reader ix

PART ONE
Pre-scripts

Pre-script 1997 3

Pre-script 2002 7

Pre-script 2009 19

Pre-script 2010 33

PART TWO

Millions of Americans' Jobs Raped by America's So-called "Leaders"!
*(Original text as written in the early 1990s
with later addenda in footnotes)*

FOREWORD by Jane Waterhouse 55

PREFACE 65

INTRODUCTION 69

CHAPTER 1...75
The Jobs Disaster!

CHAPTER 2...81
Real Jobs? Not Unless You Believe in Leprechauns,
Fantasies and the Tooth Fairy!
Or Re-Training For Non-Existent Jobs?
No Less Delusional!

CHAPTER 3...93
"Economics" Today?—Nonsense!

CHAPTER 4...105
America Works When Americans Work!
It Doesn't When They Don't!
And It Isn't Working!

CHAPTER 5...115
Incentive or Penalty for American Business? Both!

CHAPTER 6...124
American Products Mean *Real* American Jobs!

CHAPTER 7...136
The Sad and Sorry Truth of American Industry
and Its Jobs!

CHAPTER 8...156
Is There A Solution To This Jobs Disaster?
Of Course, If We Get Behind One And Make It Happen!

    1.   *Can the Positive and Negative Incentives Plan for*
        American Manufacturers/Consumers Be Sold in the
        Existing Political Situation? Nigh On To Impossible—
        But An Outside Chance! 159*

2. *Can Either Major Political Party Be Convinced that It Should Develop and Implement Its Own Real Jobs Program? Not Impossible—But the Next Thing to It!* 163

3. *A New Major Political (in a Positive Sense) Force that Cares About the Country and All the People—A Real Third Party! Possible? Absolutely! Quick Enough for the Real Jobs Crisis? Absolutely Not!* 166

4. *Is A Major Military War (Or Defense Build-Up) an Option? Quite Possibly! Although a Dreadfully Bad One in The First Instance!* 169

5. *A Passive Revolution* 173

6. *Other Prospective Solutions* 175

PART THREE
Appendices

Appendix 1: A Letter to Mr. William Clay Ford 181

Appendix 2: Detroit—Make or Break! An Outline 185

A NOTE TO THE READER

This book was originally written in the early 1990s. Unfortunately, the powers-that-were at the time, both in the United States and Europe, made its publication impossible. As you can see from its title, the book stepped on too many toes of the great and powerful who were taking the world down the garden path and didn't want to be found out.

During the ensuing years, other attempts were made to publish the book, but, for the same reason given above, these attempts have been unsuccessful. No publisher contacted in the United States or Europe has been willing to take the book on. It would appear that they are beholden to the very people the book singles out as the culprits.

The message of the book was valid and pertinent when it was originally written, and it is even more valid and pertinent today. Each time a subsequent attempt was made to publish the book (1997, 2002, and 2009), the author wrote a "pre-script" (like a "post-script," but to appear in the front of the book) to the original text in order to address the current situation of the economy.

The fourth pre-script, written in 2010, deals with the cataclysm facing our nation right now, with some thoughts about how such an economic hurricane came about, overtook us, and now has our nation by the throat. This pre-script suggests a way of making our nation whole again if we hurry. It is a strategy that has been developed since the original book was written. The action course proposed is the most desirable, although there are other worthy possibilities in the original book.

The four pre-scripts to this book are important for the book's value to you. I believe that you will agree. The situation of the economy is reflected at each of the separate dates when the pre-scripts were written. All four give worthy perspectives at the times of their writing, because economic conditions varied from one time to the other. So, please read these pre-scripts. They make some crucial points.

All the pre-scripts can be found in Part One of this book. Part Two contains the original text as written in the early 1990s (with a few footnotes containing text that was added later). Part Three contains the appendices. Unless otherwise indicated, sources for all figures cited in this book are either the U.S. Department of Commerce or the U.S. Department of Labor.

It is my hope that you and other readers will be moved by the words in this book to rally by one means or another so that together we can rebuild the American Dream instead of unwittingly and unfairly being conned into contributing to its tragic burial.

PART ONE
PRE-SCRIPTS

PRE-SCRIPT
1997

JOB CREATION? (YES)
WHAT KIND OF JOBS? (DON'T ASK!)

These words are being written in mid-November 1997. The Administration's "job creation" figure for its time in the White House ranges from 11,000,000 to 13,000,000, depending upon the source of the information, the day, the time, maybe even the weather. Undoubtedly jobs have been added. How many is obviously debatable, and who added those jobs is even less clear.

However, the real issues are not these claims. Rather, they are:

- the jobs lost—number
- the jobs added—or claimed to have been added
- the average pay of jobs lost
- the average pay of jobs added
- the types of jobs lost
- the types of jobs added
- the number of jobs required by an average household to support a four-person family at a defined level— prior to this Administration (as well as in earlier decades)

- the number of jobs required by an average household to support a four-person family at the same defined level—in the present time

It would also be useful to know how many jobs have been lost from our country, as a result of so-called outsourcing to the Pacific Rim, the "Asian Tigers," Southeast Asia, Latin America, South America, the Caribbean and so on.

The sorry truth is that answers to these questions are not to be had. The media will not pursue the answers and are easily satisfied with glib, pre-packaged talking points. The Administration puts out mountains of figures that do not answer the questions, and this is deliberate. They don't want us to know. One woman employee of the Department of Labor's Bureau of Labor Statistics said in a radio street interview, "Don't pay any attention to the figures—we change them any way we want!" This is hardly reassuring. It is certainly not helpful or useful. Where, then, are we to turn with our questions?

A noted academic at a highly prestigious university made very clear that, although he had come up with some answers, he could not make them public. He said that he was too young to have his career aborted and his family's income imperiled. Conclude what you will.

These days, politicians, tragically, are seldom either statesmen or people known for their honesty. So, as sources for such volatile information, they would be a little less than credible even if they could get their hands on valid data, which is highly doubtful.

Answers will thus have to be pieced together from bits of information gathered here and there. Beyond this writer's own immediate experience and simple observations, there are sufficient facts from government documents, facts presented later in this book, to lead to the determination that the dire nature of the situation is incontrovertible. There are also the numbers from a well-known, highly respected management school professor (who wishes not to be identified because of this book's negative potential for his career—contributors to his institution being likely to become alienated since many of them are targets of these pages). The numbers corroborate the facts without the shadow of a doubt. More important than all else, however, is the realization that the utter devastation involved is a matter not simply of numbers on a piece of paper but of the lives of *real* people and their families—millions of them!

The final decades of this century have seen a lot of endings—from the tearing down of the Berlin Wall, to the "crumbling" of Communism. Here at home, we've witnessed the death of many major industries...the demise of the family farm system...and the end of the period during which our country was the leader in virtually all aspects of the world's future. Doomsayers tell us these signs indicate that the ever better standard of living we as Americans have enjoyed for more than a hundred years is also nearing an end. But it does not have to be so. It must not be so!

This book is meant as a beginning to stop that end. More than ever, America needs the brainpower and creativity of its people. Letting a small percentage of our people determine the future will no longer do. It will take all of us—collectively contributing and working to our utmost—to get us back to where we were. Success starts with one individual. And then another. And another. Together, our combined brainpower is stronger than any challenge we face. We must recapture the American Dream—with its self-respect, respect for others, respect for our nation, and respect for the American way of life (with good jobs to support it).

PRE-SCRIPT
2002

U.S. JOBS OR FOREIGN "STUFF"?

This addendum to the original book is being written in January, 2002. The book was finished and ready for publication in the mid-nineties. There was no way to get it published at the time; it simply stepped on too many greedy connivers' prospects for lining their own pockets. Since one conniver depended on the other—numerous publishers, for example, on banks and financial interests—the boycott was iron-bound not only in the United States but in Europe as well, where they were no less beholden to the denizens of the financial netherworld.

There is no field in which it can be said that all of the people are base in nature and without scruples. There are many good people at the top of organizations, as well as at all levels; the problem is that there are simply not enough of them. Unfortunately and unhappily, the rat-catchers predominate, be it on Wall Street, in the media, politics, law firms, corporations, accounting organizations—and on and on throughout the spectrum of those who affect our lives.

Would that it were not so, but it is! The worst of the lot are too often at the top, calling the shots and thereby setting the course for their enterprises. Down at the bottom and in between usually are good people, certainly not all, but most.

They simply follow the orders of the so-called leaders (or lose their jobs), usually without realizing the damage being done to others' lives.

The fact is that millions of jobs lost today can be traced to millions of jobs raped yesterday by our erstwhile "leaders"!

The basic issue today is the same as it was back in the early 1990s when this book was first written—jobs! Two dire problems have befallen us recently, but out of darkness light is born (e.g., day follows night, bright summer replaces dark winter). So, let's hope that these disasters awaken us to a new dawn.

The horror of September 11, 2001 and the present recession are basically the result of the same two problems. The first of these is the failure to monitor our country's policies, as perceived throughout the rest of the world and as they are affecting our country here at home, by our presidential administrations going back several decades. The second problem, and one that is no less serious, is the failure in oversight on the same two counts by our Congress during the same period.

Job losses were an inevitable result of the Reagan administration's decree that this country was to become a high-tech society and, with a service economy, was to enter the post-industrial era. Subsequent policies drove out relatively high-paying manufacturing jobs. and replaced them with low-paying service—retail, clerical, fast-food, and other non-manufacturing—jobs. Most of the manufacturing jobs were literally destroyed.

Making *things* (manufacturing) makes sense and real jobs. Making *comparatively nothing* makes nonsense and perishable jobs (services). Certainly neither a manufacturing economy nor a service economy (or even a combination of the two) is without risk. However, the risk is far lower in a manufacturing economy (assuming a rational mix of products) than in one based essentially on services. This conclusion is valid particularly if we have jobs making things first for our own use and consumption, *then* for sale to the export market.

As it stands, however, we cannot make even some of the products that are needed to prosecute the war against the terrorists in Afghanistan (no—not black berets from China!). Being unable to supply our military totally from our own shores is just plain dangerous for our defense, not to mention damaging to our *real* jobs availability (relatively high-paying manufacturing jobs)!

Should we depend upon former, as well as potential, enemies for some of the products necessary to protect ourselves, because we no longer can or do make them? Don't think so!

Russia and China and others of similar stripe don't exactly inspire great confidence as suppliers of critical materials for our future peace and well-being. With apologies to our State and Commerce Departments (their jobs are not easy), convoluted logic often turns out to be less than logical. In this case, the convoluted logic puts cheap consumer prices and good bilateral relations over good jobs for Americans and reliable sources for our defense needs. When you go up a busy one-way street that is supposed to be down only, it doesn't really matter which side of the street you use. Generally, there is only one result—a god-almighty crash!

Back to the Reagan years. President Reagan did many vitally important things for this country, such as furthering high-tech development, restoring patriotism, rebuilding our defense capability, facing down the Soviet Union, rejuvenating our faith in ourselves as a nation, and more. However, there are important questions associated with the effects of Reagan Administration policies on *real* jobs for the American people and on the maintenance of our essential manufacturing base. Here are some of the questions raised at the time and the responses provided by a major figure in the Reagan administration. (Responses, while not reported verbatim, capture the essence of the answers.)

"How many millions of Americans will be unemployed by this move to a high-tech society?"
"We don't know."
"For how long will they be unemployed?"
"We have no way of estimating the time."

"What will people who lose their jobs do in what may be twenty or more years of transition?"
"We will help with re-training."

"How much money will be required for re-training?"
"Hard to say."

"Well, it will surely require billions of dollars. Where will this money come from?"
"We haven't determined that yet"

"How do you expect to re-train (for employment) people who are older? People who are not educated? People who—for whatever reason—are not suitable for re-training? People who would not be hired regardless of training for reasons of background, unsavory records, and so forth?"
"We don't know."

Hardly reassuring answers to critical questions!

The questions were asked a little more than twenty years ago. What we have seen since is many people working two or three jobs to keep families going on a desperate survival basis; NAFTA, under the Clinton administration, siphoning more and more jobs out of this country; job "globalization" and "free markets" under the Reagan, Bush I, Clinton, and Bush II administrations compounding the job losses like a jet vacuum cleaner sucking sand from the ocean floor. More of the same is to come from another free trade agreement covering the entire Western hemisphere unless it is stopped.

So, what was set in motion a couple of decades ago tragically has come to pass. *Real* jobs in too great numbers have disappeared; cheap (non-manufacturing) jobs have swelled. Low- and moderate-income people have been hurt severely. Wall Street, corporations, and people in their upper ranks, along with people who had money to "invest" or to risk, by and large, did incredibly well (if they were on the inside track). On the other hand, those not on the inside track took a bath on the "old economy" and were blown away by the dot coms, the "new economy." The "players" continue to play and make lots of money whether the markets go up or down, whether mergers and acquisitions are few or many, even when bankruptcies multiply at a frightening rate. These same people buy solid enterprises for ridiculously low prices, because such companies have gotten into cash trouble (their balance sheets having been decimated).

Once again, let's retrace our steps back to the Reagan economic policies, the seedbed of new billionaires and, at the other extreme, rapidly rising numbers of people fighting to keep body and soul (and family) together with too many jobs paying too little money. When a household can't meet its needs with one income, both parents have to work, and the family pays a high price with children frequently left on their own ("latch-key kids"). The society suffers because its children begin to lose a sense of values, as do—and possibly even to a greater extent—their parents. This cycle goes on, repeating itself with each new generation.

The Reagan Administration policies created more and more of these high-risk family situations—too many jobs required in one family to make sheer survival into what is called a living. This tragic problem was the result of moving jobs out of the United States to nations where labor was cheap (goodbye bricks and mortar; hello virtual world!). Another reason for the same dire consequences was the selling of our manufactured goods markets to whatever companies offered the lowest prices. Initially these companies were foreign (e.g., Japanese, and later Korean, Taiwanese, Chinese, Indonesian, etc.). U.S. companies saw in such countries, with their low labor costs, an opportunity to save money by producing in these countries both entire products (such as cars, tires, shoes, and apparel) and limitless components (such as steel, textiles, micro-chips, sub-assemblies, parts, and so on). What these U.S. companies made elsewhere, they sold to us in this country.

Thus, these American companies were able to increase their profits greatly (in simple terms: much lower cost to produce + same or even somewhat slightly lower price = higher profit). U.S. companies even shipped parts to other countries, assembled final products there, and shipped them back for sale in the United States (example, cars from Mexico). The companies did well, but what this actually meant was that millions of *real* U.S. jobs were lost to other countries.

These economic and market changes were accepted by most Americans for one the following reasons. First, most people didn't understand the real losses to our country (because "most people" weren't the people who lost their jobs and didn't know anybody who was devastated in this way). Second, the only thing most people saw was that they were paying lower prices for the (now imported) things they bought—cars, shoes, clothes, computers, TVs, practically any and everything they needed or thought they did. The suffering of their fellow citizens was either unseen or rationalized away. Third, and worst of all, the societal pressure to "have it all" convinced them that having an SUV or a bigger house or whatever was important. It was more important than anything, even if it meant having Mom and Dad working three or four or more jobs—while the kids initially were in daycare and later fended for themselves—instead of one or the other being at home taking care of those kids!

The results for our nation, as I see them, assuredly in differing ways and degrees, are less than healthy and—overall, in too many respects—destructive of the society's fundamental values, ethics, and moral fiber. In short, "stuff" is taking over people's lives and displacing the basics of family life, along with people's loyalties and many forms of support for each other.

This new economic structure, along with the financial "magic" involved, has led to the accumulation of large sums of money by many organizations and certain people. Much of this money and new technology were invested in the "new economy." The "old economy," making things in brick and mortar structures here in our own backyard and selling such things, was passé. So, out of nowhere and in relatively no time (with a few exceptions) came the dot coms.

Whether or not these dot coms had business plans that made sense, or whether they made profits, was irrelevant. Wall Street, and the financial community as a whole, saw a bonanza in the offing and beat the drum of greed literally to death, so that in due course there emerged what was called the "dot com bubble." As with all bubbles, it burst! With it went millions of jobs and trillions of dollars in bewitched investors' money.

So, because of this economic delusion and the horror of September 11, our great country is in recession, if not worse, thanks to greed and tragedy. The U.S. economy is affecting that of much of the rest of the world; this will make a return to economic health far more difficult. Jobs here and elsewhere in the developed countries—let alone in the third world—will be in dire and dangerous straits for the immediate future, if not longer.

These two traumatic events—the maniacal horrors of 9/11 and our economic difficulties—were the result, in the final analysis, of presidential administrations failure to monitor both our government's operations in intelligence, which should have prevented September 11, and operations in the financial sector, which should have prevented the dot com bubble, not to mention the bursting of that bubble. No less responsible or guilty—and maybe even more so—is our legislative branch of government, which failed in carrying out the oversight for which it is responsible. These traumas could and should have been prevented.

September 11 clearly involved all of our intelligence organizations: the FBI, the Immigration and Naturalization Service, the Customs Service, the State Department, and probably a number of others. With respect to the dot com disaster, the S.E.C., the Treasury Department, the Federal Reserve, and certainly others were culpable. However, the ultimate responsibility rests with the presidential administrations and U.S. congresses. They abjectly failed the people of this country. Unfortunately, presidential administrations and the U.S. congresses will never be held to account, despite the fact that they clearly had numerous credible warnings over an extended period of time and yet were totally remiss in not protecting this nation and its citizens from either catastrophe.

Worse still, a number of disreputable people have capitalized on one or the other, if not both, of these tragic events. Even though the book that follows was written in the early part of the 1990s, what it says unhappily still applies at the beginning of this new millennium. In fact, on many counts the situation is even worse today. The publication of this book, as mentioned earlier, was blocked at the time of its writing and has been ever since for obvious reasons—the most apparent being that the publishers involved in one way or another were beholden to the very people assailed on its pages.

At this time in our lives, January of 2002, Enron is yet one more case of dereliction in monitoring and oversight by the various agencies of this administration and by the present Congress, and earlier ones in both instances as well. Again, employees and investors have been devastated. Worst of all, however, employees have seen their pensions and, it appears, their 401(K)s either destroyed or drastically reduced in the process of this bankruptcy, the largest in the nation's history. Greed and, in this case, possible fraud and accounting dereliction, along with audit irregularities—if not worse—have been at the heart of this financial collapse. At a minimum, Wall Street and other financial interests had a hand in the situation, if for no other reason than utterly irresponsible stock promotion. So, once more, where was the monitoring by the administration's agencies concerned and the oversight of the Congress?

The point being made here is that this book, written in the early part of the last decade, unfortunately still applies as far as jobs, Wall Street, corporations, and the government are concerned. The tragedy of it all is that the United States has had another horrible disaster inflicted upon it. The events of September 11, 2001 can clearly and unmistakably be seen as barbaric. Our jobs loss not so! They did not take place in one day. The effects were spread out over time and affected millions of people. The loss of jobs was not as soul-searing or as riveting for an entire nation as was 9/11—yet, its ultimate impact has been devastating, in some respects (with vastly greater numbers affected) even more calamitous.

The horrors of 9/11 are galvanizing and inerasable. Whether the ultimate effect of one calamity is greater than the other, however, is still to be seen. In some ways one appears to be the basis for the other. The greed of some in this country has led to a view of the United States among certain elements in other countries that, at best, has been damaging to our interests, and at worst, may have inspired the terrorism that confronts us.

Which of these two terrible blows to our country is worse really isn't an issue. They both are dire. Regardless, effective monitoring by our presidential administrations* and conscientious oversight by our U.S. congresses should, and I believe, could have prevented one or both! We need to find and elect the right people to do the right job for the future of this wonderful country and its people. Not easy, but there are ways to do it better than we are. For instance, objective comparisons on a simple "yes" or "no" basis by each candidate for all major issues would help enormously.

Democracy cannot really work if we do not know for what we are voting, and most of us don't, despite our protestations otherwise! The polls, TV, and the two parties tell us what we are supposed to think. That is bad, as one can readily see, because they tell us only what they want us to hear. Real campaign reform, feasible media access, and inclusion on a valid basis of other parties' candidates in TV debates would be good starters.

If we do not know where our representatives stand on manufacturing in this country, we can face disaster for the nation—a devastating loss of *real* jobs. What happens when U.S. manufacturing jobs are replaced by service jobs (because manufacturing jobs have been moved out of the United States to other countries) is that our workers are paid less (service jobs) and generally have to work several jobs (as many as three or four in a family) to sustain the family on a survival basis. How-

---

*The U.S. Government departments and agencies involved in September 11, for example, would include the FBI and each and every intelligence organization, the Immigration and Naturalization Service, and the State Department; in addition there would be entities of the Defense, Treasury, Justice, Energy, Transportation, Health and Human Services Departments and any others that might have a role (even Education—e.g., in foreign student tracking).

ever, such U.S. corporations, their key executives, and investors make unreasonable and undeserved amounts of money.

The reason is simple. Cheap labor and lower costs generally (e.g., subsidies, few if any anti-pollution requirements, etc.) abroad mean lower costs for these corporations. Prices are maintained or, possibly, reduced here in the United States. The obvious result is higher profits even with a price reduction. Consequently, investors and key executives, plus all those involved in the manipulation of stock prices and similar depredations upon our people, make inordinate and outrageous amounts of money. The rest of the people, the vast majority, pay the piper, that is, the bill for these relatively few people getting sickeningly large amounts of dollars at our expense.

These predators basically make three arguments:

1. Americans have more jobs (in what is essentially a service economy). True—more jobs, *but* jobs that pay less, so people have to work several jobs with the result that families are being rent asunder and basic values annihilated.

2. Americans pay less for what they buy. True—for most imported goods from foreign companies; *but* not always true for imported goods that are made or assembled by U.S. companies abroad and sold here as American products. The inflationary rate could not continue to go up each year were it otherwise, even with the increase of prices for services and products, such as they are, that still originate or are produced here.

3. Americans (half of the nation) invest in the stock market. True, but it's mostly passive or indirect—through funds or other financial instruments, with the investments made by the financial people running them. Their pension funds and 401(K)s

whose values are related to corporate profits benefit to some degree—if they are job holders whose companies provide such perks; more and more companies do not. Nevertheless, their relative income compared to that of key corporate executives, investors, financial organizations, corporate law firms, and so on is miniscule; the average job holder makes only a tiny fraction of such people's incomes. For example, many corporate chief executives make tens of millions of dollars a year and some investors even far more.

So, what is it to be—U.S. jobs or foreign "stuff"? There can be only one answer for Americans who care about other Americans and believe in our country's basic values. A choice? Yes! An alternative? No!

PRE-SCRIPT
2009

FACING THE WORST ECONOMIC CRISIS
IN DECADES

Now—FINALLY—jobs are being seen as important by our so-called "leaders" of recent times, by their new replacements, and, ostensibly at least, even by some holdovers who might be numbered among the worst of the lot. But are they *real* jobs or the straw men (and women) projects of political expediency?

This preface is being written on Sunday, February 15, 2009—irony of ironies!—exactly two months to the day on which we owe our government taxes that approximate five months' worth of our previous year's labors.

As a result of the dire and critical situation in which the United States finds itself (and the absolute chaos it has caused around the world), much at last is being made of the millions of jobs lost. And, God knows, rightly so. However, no one talks about the vastly greater number of people in families affected by these losses. On average, there must be at least four people in every family devastated by each such job eliminated. Those losses mean *people*, hurt terribly in many different ways, not just statistics. The "numbers" are really tragedies of limitless kinds for enormous groups of our fellow human beings, our neighbors, not to mention ourselves if we are among those who have been the victims of various cost-cutting measures referred to in euphemisms—or, to put it more harshly, axed!

The job losses we have experienced are actually the worst in memory since the Great Depression, by far worse than any "recession" without doubt (despite some claims to the contrary). These losses are infinitely beyond the staggering "statistics." In one way or another they severely hurt everyone in this nation as a result of lost homes, lost home values, lost pensions, lost incomes, lost investments, and lost schooling, to mention but a few with the list being virtually without end.

Those responsible are the crooks repeatedly cited in this book—major elements in Wall Street, corporations, *our* government (too many administrations and congresses), and many more of their ilk—all interlocked and involved in one way or another with the nefarious activities that have caused this tragic situation. Yet few, if any, will be held to account and thrown in the slammer. Some will be charged in civil court and make settlements. Most will go scot-free.

Worse still, they are, to a large extent, the very same people (the financial moguls) that our government is saving with our money—and without even a blush on either part. The worst they have experienced has been a few embarrassing questions at Congressional hearings—and all sickeningly for the benefit of a few frustrated thespian politicians who substitute the hearings for their thwarted ambitions in the acting fraternity. In many cases the questioners, pretending sanctity, are equally guilty, being the very people who totally failed in their responsibility for oversight of these same financial institutions, and worse.

Sordidly, it is these blackguards together (the Wall Streeters and their abettors) who have spread this financial virus throughout the world. It is their greed that has caused chaos across the entire earth. Such depravity has been carried tragically to all quarters of the planet by American institutions in one way or another. Unfortunately, their overtures found willing foreign ears, people eager to cooperate and thus no less culpable.

These financial wizards have actually taken over our nation, and far beyond, with their swindling ways. Even more tragic, we have gone from being a country that made things to being a country that by comparison makes very little, except bad deals and electronic money transfers. The dirty deal of financial mumbo-jumbo has taken over from the clean deal of producing and selling goods that we, and people in the rest of the world, need if we are to have a viable way of life. This country has become hostage to a bunch of hustlers. Just consider what is at the heart of this mess—the banking "industry" and the so-called financial services "industry" which includes, I guess, all the other purveyors of "Quick Willy" double-talk as well as "Slick Willy" sleaze.

Are there any good banks and reputable financial organizations left? No doubt there are. Are there still honorable people in these disgraced dens of infamy? Of course there are, but far too few of them are found at the top of such organizations. The saddest part of all in these once hallowed halls of finance is that a lot of good young people and a lot of not-so-young innocents were trapped into these "industries" by people with no conscience but with buckets full of money. Such shameless rotters ensnared too many decent people who were seeking simply what they thought was "the good life." These decent people were the pathetic victims of the avaricious core who romanticized them into their iniquitous snares of endless bonuses and $2,500 bottles of wine!

Incredibly enough, with all the hue and cry about lost jobs and an economy in disaster, there is no talk about the real basis for the whole mess—an economy once soundly based on a solid manufacturing infrastructure that has virtually been destroyed, with most of what is left having been taken over by a bunch of financial manipulators and charlatans. Worse still is the apparent acceptance of the assumption that such a manufacturing base has been lost forever and simply cannot be restored. If that were true, which it isn't, our country would be lost. However, unless our government has enough courage and brains to secure the return of manufacturing to this country through what I call a "Fair Trade Equalization Formula" (see below, in the section entitled "Pre-Script 2010") or in some other way, in my opinion and that of a number of realistic economists, the United States will become a second-rate country at best and quite likely worse. The policy dilemma and foreign political ramifications of our enormous overseas debt conflicting with the restoration of manufacturing in the United States (reduced imports from China, particularly, but also from others) are not unrecognized or ignored here. They are dealt with in what follows.

The restoration of manufacturing means the restoration of *real* jobs and much more, such as being able to produce the means for our own defense as well as other things critical to our nation's needs. The jobs assuredly must have at least two characteristics: (1) they must be sustaining, not temporary or one-shot; (2) they must be well-paying (with income that is fair and sufficient to provide for a family's needs). Why? It's basic! The foundation for a consumer economy essentially is: Jobs = Income = Consumer Purchases, Investments, Savings, and Taxes to sustain needed government operations.

No jobs, no income, no purchases, no economy. "No jobs" is not realistic. High unemployment is. So, too, are jobs with inadequate income. It all adds up to a shattered economy and the likelihood of grave civil problems.

Since this book was originally written back in the early 1990s, there has been one major change—but one only—that I would like to cite. I hope that it does not sound like a whitewash, because it certainly isn't intended to be one. On the other hand, it is a partial justification for the outsourcing and off-shoring done by some CEOs, most often in manufacturing companies, who were left with no choice competitively if their companies were to survive.

At the same time, this off-shoring of jobs is an even greater condemnation of Wall Street as well as the government's most recent administrations and congresses going back to the beginning of the Reagan regime primarily, but possibly even a little earlier in some quarters of the government and financial communities. In the first instance, Wall Street forced off-shoring for company profits. With regard to the latter two, our administrations and congresses, they were utterly and unconscionably derelict in not providing incentives/disincentives (or some other means) to avert deterioration of the economy. Thus the problem grew exponentially in the intervening years.

Too many chief executive officers of corporations—primarily manufacturing although by no means exclusive of other businesses—were unquestionably greedy. (Fortunately some—not nearly enough—were anything but and have fought the good fight here.) However, that greed was force-fed by Wall Street avarice demanding ever greater profits at least quarterly. This combination of greedy CEOs and avaricious Wall Streeters was further abetted by numerous administrations/congresses doing absolutely nothing to protect the American worker. In fact, often the opposite

As a result, the only way to meet the ever more pressing demands for profits was to go off-shore or out of the country for cheap labor. Then came the importing of low-priced talent and skills. Initially, foreign labor was obtained outside the U.S. for manufacturing, and then later for providing services (financial backroom work, telemarketing, customer service aid by telephone from India, Timbuktu, or some other end of the earth)—labor that was available on the cheap as a way to improve bottom-line profitability. The importing of inexpensive capabilities for U.S. jobs was a later device of the devils. Sometimes it was legitimate because of a lack of qualified Americans to do those jobs. Sometimes it wasn't—more times than warranted!

Often slave-labor wages, no pollution controls, various kinds of foreign government subsidies, and other rank practices furthered Wall Street–fed greed for profit to which too many CEOs fell prey. Such foreign cost advantages were highly detrimental to American workers' ability to compete with foreign production. In most situations it was impossible!

Even worse was the utter dereliction of the U.S. congresses of those times, not to mention the several administrations, in allowing well-known U.S. companies with household brand names to produce off-shore and then sell those products back into the United States, still the world's single largest consumer market, and to do so at exorbitant profits. Globalization became a buzz word that sanctified the do-nothing syndrome of our legislative and executive branches of government to sacrifice American workers for cheap product prices. The subterfuge that cheap prices for Chinese products didn't destroy the U.S. economy was the insidious way to ever greater profits for the ever greedier bloodsuckers. The rationalization was simply that the benefit of low-price goods for U.S. consumers was a testament to globalization and to hell with the cost of lost jobs! And devastated families!

Many companies, old and new, became nothing more than importers—producing everything outside of the United States and selling it all back into this country at great profit because of cheap foreign production costs, subsidies, and distorted exchange rates.. As just mentioned, the ruse here was that American consumers could satisfy their needs and desires at lower prices. While this was true in too many cases, the cost was actually very high in terms of lost jobs.

In due course, as we have experienced again and even more seriously in this round—which has been far worse than at any time since the 1930s—lost jobs lead to lost income. Lost income in turn leads to lost purchases (and taxes too, by the way), which then lead to lost profits and, finally, to recession or worse. Unfortunately it's a vicious cycle that feeds on itself. Consumers who still have income (not wealth) perpetuate the problem by reducing their spending. They do so through saving and fewer purchases in order to protect themselves against unforeseen eventualities. To restore the trust in government (as well as in the financial and allied organizations) required to rebuild the economy is a monumental task!

Unfortunately, the Wall Street fixation with profit and greed, in my opinion, led to a culture in this country that wound up with the greed for money pervading the entire nation. Greedy mortgage sellers and greedy banks that packaged those sub-prime mortgages (backed by abysmal or non-existent credit ratings or, worse still, made on the basis of what many making the loans themselves called "liar loans") then sold them to mostly unsuspecting buyers worldwide. Some people who obtained mortgages—in fact I believe most—were taken into camp by unscrupulous brokers and the like deliberately selling a bill of goods (impossible variable rate interest escalations, no down payments, no credit worthy investigations, etc.). Unfortunately some (a small percentage based on what I can find out) were probably culpable in the belief that they could flip (buy and sell) properties for large profits. Some were looking to benefit on the assumption that the real estate market rise would be endless and they could always refinance to their advantage (covering outrageous mortgage escalations, pulling cash out of their house investment if desired and probably numerous other reasons). Such people probably could be considered culpable, but not in any sense to the same degree as the bankers, brokers, and flippers.

So, my conclusion is that outsourcing, combined with mortgage misrepresentations, led us to our current disaster of economic chaos in lost jobs and unimaginable national debt. Clearly responsible are Wall Street, the lack of controls by the U.S. Government (administrations and congresses) and the greed of many CEOs. Not all, but too many of the latter, were forced by Wall Street and government sins of omission and commission into the outsourcing and off-shoring (not to mention the insourcing of cheap foreign skills) in which they engaged to an appalling and frightening degree. The destruction of our manufacturing base leaves us highly vulnerable to the economic chaos confronting us now and the inability of this country to make even what is necessary for our very own defense needs.

In the final analysis, the takeover of this country by financial organizations has led not only to our nation's turmoil but that of the entire world. Why the world too? Simply because these self-same financial organizations peddled greediness and the mechanisms to achieve the goal of inordinate profit through Wall Street magic on a world-wide scale.

Worst of all, nobody in the political swim of Washington wants to discuss, much less do anything, with regard to our lost manufacturing base. If action isn't taken to restore *this* infrastructure, assuming that our country survives the current disaster, the swindlers will reassume control, and the entire debacle will be repeated. However, it will be done with a "reform" face that makes the current picture look legitimate and safe. It will be the exact opposite—crooked and, sooner or later, disastrous! In the hope that we are lucky enough to come out at the other end of this disastrous economic tunnel, let us smarten up and refuse to have a curtain of deceit and out-and-out fraud blind us to what could be Armageddon the next time.

We must not be so foolish as to let this happen again if, by some miracle, we are able to save the bacon this time. I hope and pray that we can, but realistically it will take nothing short of that miracle! The World Trade Center tragedy was a horror.

The current economic catastrophe is in some ways worse. Terrorism comes in many forms and with many different faces. We did not let the terror attack *on* the Twin Towers, the heart of the world's financial center, stop us. We should not, and cannot, let the more disguised attack *of* that center's basic financial organizations—run by our own citizens, sickeningly—attack on our own country do so at this point or any other.

What a terrible irony: the target of the World Trade Center airliner attack again has become the focus for the source of this nation's and the world's agony. That first attack sadly affected thousands of people; this one ravages millions upon millions. The World Trade Center losses were avenged by strong military action. In the current tragedy with horrific fall-out, the avengers are dancing the two-step with the perpetrators. We are bailing out, instead of jailing, the criminals at the root of this catastrophe. The financial system must be saved, including—as it turns out—the people responsible for its failure?! There is something radically wrong in this temporizing with such malevolent evil. Does changing this approach of saving the bacon through protecting those who executed the slaughter require a miracle? Probably!

However, we at least can help reduce future damage with more effective preventive measures. We should begin by replacing the malefactors with qualified people, to be sure, but do everything possible to make certain that these new people are not only competent but also honorable. It should be possible to fix some of the damage caused by the previous greedy, grasping cheats and thieves through throwing out such blackguards. So, believe in this miracle (a lesser one than the first one but a miracle regardless) and pray hard for the next one. It is to have the right people, in the right places, at the right times!

Apologies for repeating, at least in part, some of what has been said before. However, it is important that the vital points not be lost in a lot of words from my strongly held (impassioned may be a better word) views. So, I hope that you will grant me this leeway to mention again what to me are some of the critical considerations. They are restated for clarity but also, and more important, for emphasis.

As stated at the very beginning of this pre-script (and it is the most essential point of all), jobs finally became important to those so-called leaders who preceded the new administration of 1/20/09. Tragically, only disaster forced their attention to this issue. These culprits included many (if not most) of the major actors in the previous administrations and congresses, financial institutions, multi-national corporations and many others as well. Ironically, they can still be found in decision-making positions, because many of those highly culpable people are still at their same jobs in the Congress, government departments, banks, financial enterprises, the business community, and lots of other places as well.

Clearly, in the new administration of President Obama jobs are a massive consideration for the newcomers and now contradictorily, to be sure, for the holdovers in such places as the Senate and the House of Representative. Distressingly and unconscionably, many previously in the Senate, House, financial world, business, and elsewhere ignored the issue of jobs entirely, preferring to take refuge in unemployment figures cooked in similar fashion to the "accounting" books.

However, despite all the current concern and effort regarding the saving and creation of jobs, my continuing fear is that this emphasis on the issue of jobs is solely the result of jobs being lost at an alarming rate and in great numbers. If this tide of layoffs can be stemmed and in time reversed, will we find that too many of the created jobs are of a short-term nature (e.g., an infrastructure project on finishing a bridge) and thus not ongoing employment of a continuing kind or, worse still, just straw men (and women) jobs of political expedience to arrest the tide of economic disaster?

There is no doubt that the present rate of economic collapse must be reversed if this nation is to survive in any form like that of its former self. Nevertheless, what is of equal importance is to create as many *real* jobs as possible, jobs that will not end abruptly but continue on in a virtually endless sense, such as jobs making products that are needed or desired in the long run. No less important is that incomes be fair.

There is no question, on the other hand, about first things being first. We need to stop the bleeding (even with temporary or short-term jobs), but then sew up the wound (with *real* and long-term jobs), making things required in our country and elsewhere in the world—with jobs that will not go away. Doing so is what built this great nation. Letting flim-flammers take us over with promises of financial nirvana forever is what has us in the very deep hole of the moment. Clearly the machine that built this country is broken. So we must fix the fundamental problem, and not be misled by temporary jobs that help for the moment but aren't long-term solutions. Nonetheless, we must hold the dike together in order to rebuild it (short term to reach the long term).

Here are the major concerns for me at this point.

(1) Short term—Stop the avalanche of job losses by short-term means necessary and *start* rebuilding the economy with long-term job creation.

(2) Long term—Recognize that an economic structure based on consumer purchases cannot be constructed from a house of cards (or a shell game of financial manipulation). If it is, when the wind rages and the cards are blown away, jobs will disappear, income will dwindle, and therefore purchases of anything (from China, other foreign sources or the U.S.) will be reduced to a disastrous level.

(3) Long term—Also, realize that only jobs based on a manufacturing foundation (plus, of course, our natural resources and agricultural production) for products needed here and abroad (with changes

based on ongoing innovation and invention, to be sure) can provide sustainable income and accordingly ongoing purchases for a thriving economy underpinned by consumer buying. I appreciate the dilemma of having China and Japan hold a significant part of the national debt with the apparent conflicting interest of restoring the U.S. manufacturing base. However, a reasonable equalization formula should solve the problem *fairly* (not only for the U.S. but the world as well, including China in its own market and diversification of its foreign markets) despite the inevitable complaints from many directions, including certain U.S. interests. If implemented wisely, however, this strategy not only could be put in place but will also make an essential contribution to this nation's having a future worthy of itself. That has been, and is, the simple formula which produced the American standard of living for the realization of our American dreams! Once more, the basic formula: *real* jobs = *fair* income = purchasing *power* = economic *stability* = American Dream!

So, I hope and pray that these concerns may be recognized and acted on by our new administration. It is my fervent wish that I am right this time in the belief that the administration does see the validity of what is outlined here. No less, in fact even more, do I wish that, lo those many years ago when this book was written, it had been wrong about the critical jobs situation then (and certainly even more so now). Horrifyingly, it was not—the warning was only too true. Tragically, the current disaster should, and I believe could, have been averted—*but* only if this country had returned to manufacturing *real* products (not financial "products") and foreclosed a takeover of the nation by the banks and Wall Street! (It is interesting to note that the fastest growing economies in the world today are manufacturing economies—China and India.)

Would the present trauma actually have been forestalled? Possibly not, because at that point the crooks were riding high in every respect and the support they were getting was practically universal. They were seen as champions of eternal pots of gold at the ends of everlasting rainbows (a vision that they reinforced at every opportunity, not the least being non-stop commercial messages barraging eyes and ears, hearts and minds everywhere). They were aided and abetted by their complicit supporters from knaves in government (U.S. and foreign) all the way to the unprincipled hucksters of sub-prime mortgages, with innumerable other conscienceless culprits contributing to ultimate economic devastation.

At the time when this book was originally written and for many years after that, anyone holding the views expressed here was doomed to being considered either insane or not of sound mind, and possibly even a candidate for being drawn and quartered. The statements expressed herein would have been drowned out by the hue and cry for globalization (free, *but not fair*, trade) from the avaricious profiteers and those to whom they had sold their bill of goods (a lot of baloney!), not to mention the very souls of those self-same scoundrels! Their utter greed for themselves was without concern for the damage being done to millions of American families, the American way of life, or the general well-being of this nation's present and future. Treason? Yes, in my opinion! At the very least sedition. Is economic terrorism any less lethal than physical terrorism? No, as I see it, because economic terrorism causes long drawn-out suffering, and worse, affects a vast number of people (tens of millions).

The terrible truth is that the people of this country (and elsewhere) never had a chance to hear the warnings in this book, since the power structure of the time made disseminating these views impossible, preventing the book from being available to those who might read it by ensuring it was not published. My own belief is that if Americans had heard the truth, they would have had the opportunity of doing what was necessary to prevent what has transpired—certainly the worst economic crisis in decades and possibly in our history! (For the truth to have been heard broadly enough throughout the land would have required far more than just this book, but it might have served as a catalyst to get the message out.) What we are experiencing could, and should, have been avoided, had it not been for the greed and power of our so-called leaders in virtually every vital aspect of America's life.

PRE-SCRIPT
2010

OVERVIEW OF WHAT IS NEEDED
TO RESTORE A SOUND ECONOMY

The Equalization Formula for *fair* trade (discussed in part here and also later)—not free trade, which is anything but—covers many more factors than does the letter to Bill Ford of Ford Motor Company in Part Three of this book. Were our Congress interested in the well-being of our country instead of campaign contributions from our "global" corporations and various interest groups, those factors would not be academic issues. Disastrously, this Congress is not in the least bit interested in the well-being of our country, nor were previous administrations and congresses. (True of all members of administrations and congresses? Of course not! Just far too many!) If this weren't so, the current global economic disaster would not be destroying the American Dream—our jobs, our treasure, and our peace of mind, not to mention the world's regard for this nation. Such devastation is no less for most of the world's economies. Either we stand up for *real* American jobs and the return of our previous manufacturing operations (which are what created such jobs in the first place) or we sit on our hands and watch this nation follow the history of Rome onto the ash heap of history!

Anyway, some of the factors that should be addressed for *fair* trade are: slave labor rates, particularly in Asian and mid-European nations; foreign government subsidies of their industries and exports, often both; U.S. states' subsidies of foreign manufacturers' plants in this country; lack of pollution controls, as well as safety requirements, in other countries and their consequent cost elimination in prices paid by consumers; other cost differentials for foreign management in countries where our imports originate; and on and on ad nauseam. (We might also consider various tariffs and other restrictions put on our exports to these countries by their governments.)

The Equalization Formula presented here (or some other measure for the same purpose) should be applied to the products of all industries that manufacture, or once did before outsourcing, in the United States and are brought into this country for sale here. No more free rides for foreign companies or U.S. "global" corporations in the world's single largest consuming market, our United States of America.

The hue and cry of protectionism raised by such a proposal will be loud and long—from various elements in the Congress, the Administration, Wall Street, "global" corporations, U.S. importers, foreign countries and companies, not to mention Washington's K Street lobbyists and many more. The *real* workers in this country for far too long have been the fall guys for the cover-up of the special interests. All of these groups profit sickeningly, in one way or another, from the devastation of workers in our country. It is these workers who make up the true middle class that once paid the freight (personal income plus many other taxes) for this nation (and still do if *real* numbers—including what they, the middle class, create for the income of the top 1–5 percent of earners—are used).

We should insist that if American companies want to sell in the United States, they must produce here. That also goes for foreign companies that produce *some* final products here. If they want to produce elsewhere or bring in parts or components, they will be subject to the Equalization Formula. Loopholes and end-runs will not be possible—either it's made here or it's not!

For far too long the United States has been taken over by the financial deal-makers (too many of them dirty deals) of this nation who in their greed for money and power have, along with their collaborators in too many other nations, put this nation—as well as the entire world—in grave jeopardy.

If we haven't learned that egregious deals make for disaster, and that we had better get back to making things instead of letting financial manipulators destroy our very substance, the future is dire: the dump, not the Dream!

Myriad sources—many, if not most of which were mentioned earlier—will state that they were unaware of the facts of this harsh reality. The excuse, with little question, will be that the problems besetting this government were so well obscured that they were indiscernible. Unfortunately, this excuse has to do not with the obscurity of the problems but rather with the blindness of those who should have been able to see but were unable to because they were blinded by the tears of their own sardonic laughter.

Problems we have—probably even more than we realize! However, simply to consider them as insuperable without clarifying what such resignation would mean to this nation is not only unconscionable but a certain death knell!

The biggest financial issue we face is having gone from the world's largest creditor nation to its biggest debtor in a relatively few years. In the process, the United States has basically shifted from an innovative manufacturing economy to a financial services dominated crapshoot with the dice loaded for aggrandizement of the greedy. As the Reagan Administration put it: this is a post-industrial era, a high-tech society, a service economy. That formula has given rise to some warnings, not to mention utter calamities—dot com bust, Enron blow-out, housing bubble etc.—and culminated in the current U.S. and world economic disaster!

The next most difficult problem economically is that the countries which own the major part of our national debt are China and Japan. Why is this such an earth-shaking consideration? Two reasons. One, we unfortunately represent a critical market for their products. In effect, they and some others, but primarily they for now, are our new production base, and our market (selling to the U.S.) is vital to their economic interests. The second reason is that if they stopped lending money to us—money that we actually use, in large measure, to buy their products—we also would not be able to meet our own expenses as a nation. However, they too would be damaged severely. It's a two-way street.

In short, if it were a one-way street, we would be a bankrupt country—but it is not a one-way street! Were it so, that would truly put us between a rock and a hard place. The fact, nevertheless, is that we are afraid to alienate China and Japan by bringing our earlier manufacturing operations back to this country and instituting an equalization formula of some kind so that international trade is *fair*, not free.

The angry shout of protectionism would be heard from every corner of the earth. So, what do we do? If having *fair* trade and our own manufacturing base is called protectionism, then having the means to defend ourselves should be called the same thing, because that's exactly what it is—essential, but simply not the reality at this time. Why? Because we no longer can make all of our needed defense materiel at home. Too many U.S. manufacturing operations have been outsourced—far too many to potential enemies, believe it or not!

From the standpoint of our creditors, they actually would be better off in many respects, since an equalization plan would strengthen not only the U.S. economy (and its jobs base) but that of the rest of the world as well. The United States and other nations would once more be consumers for each other's products (services too). We and other countries could buy and also sell on a *fair* basis. So, strengthening the U.S. market (jobs mean consumers!) would strengthen other nations too. As a consequence, our ability to import goods would be enhanced and our ability to repay loans would be guaranteed. World stability would be far more assured.

Would there be any risk? Of course! Transition time, investment requirements, resistance from many sources are only a few of the problems. But such problems are infinitely less troubling than being in the disastrous crack of the moment, unable to make what we need to protect this country and struggling along with an economy that will not be able to return to, and then sustain, the American way of life.

Do we have an administration and a congress sufficiently realistic and courageous to protect America and its people? Not likely, since they are more interested in their own self-serving near-sighted agendas. However, this nation is ill-fated until these people, or their replacements, grasp that their real long-term interest is inextricably linked with the well-being of this nation and the jobs that make it possible. Only then can they ensure our nation's future (and their own)! We, unfortunately, are in the same boat with them, but they are the ones who are rowing. Therefore, we have to get them to see the rocks ahead before the boat is demolished and sinks. The boat is already foundering badly!

A crippled America cannot be replaced by China, India, or any other country or groups of countries in the world for that matter. Even the countries of the European Union know this simple fact of economic reality, despite their sometimes seemingly contrary actions and clear inability to acknowledge it without excruciating pain.

So, in the final analysis, we come down to a very simple, clear-cut decision. Defend our jobs and thereby our country, or kill what the Constitution created—a nation with life, liberty, and the pursuit of happiness for all—the American Dream! It's up to you and me. Which will it be? Stand up and be counted? Or fall down and be counted out!

Real jobs = income = buying power = consumer purchases, investment, and tax revenues (benefiting the United States and world economies) = the American Dream and world betterment. It's that basic—no economic "black box" or financial mumbo-jumbo!

Some people may say that the United States is still the largest producer (implying manufacturer) in the world. That was once true. However, such a statement is now highly misleading. The claim is based on data from 2007 being compared with data from a decade earlier, with twice as much being produced in 2007 than ten years previously. However, the term "producer" refers to production not just of manufactured goods but also to increases of massive proportions in "products" that are purely financial in nature. The comparison of the 2007 figure compared to that of a decade earlier fails to mention this very basic fact, the vastly greater amount of financial "products" represented in the *total* figure for 2007.

In addition, several other factors must be pointed out. First, our manufacturing base comprises a far different industry mix now than then. Furthermore, that mix was changing long before a decade ago—at least twenty or thirty years ago, if not more. The change in the mix meant some industries (essentially in major manufacturing) were being lost, and, yes, some were being created (mostly service industries, predominantly financial in one form or another with respect to the amount of dollars involved).

Second, much of what was lost was being outsourced (first manufacturing, then back-office operations, next various other service functions). In time, even a substantial amount of what was created (electronicss manufacturing, financial operations of various kinds, and other manufacturing innovations, as well as service functions) was outsourced. In addition, for some of the newly created industries, cheap labor was being brought into the United States ("insourced") to fill many of the jobs.

Third, for industries old and new, many of the parts and assemblies or components were (and continue to be) produced in foreign countries, assembled in this country, and sold here or elsewhere. For example, let's use a Japanese or American car assembled in the U.S. but with many foreign components and parts. The *total* cost of the car is included in the U.S. production number (GDP)—clearly a fantasy figure when such imported elements are included in U.S. Gross Domestic Production. Being manipulated in this way for determining the U.S. production total is not only wrong through inflating the figure for U.S. production but deliberately misleading and an utter deceit as well.

If just 30 percent of the final manufactured product (this car) is from foreign sources (probably a highly conservative estimate on average), the so-called U.S. production figure (multiplying the 30 percent of the car's cost by millions of units) is a very large amount in just one product category. Accordingly, in no way can these cars' total cost be considered an accurate reflection of U.S. output, any more than the foreign parts justifying a "made in the U.S.A." claim.

Regardless of where such cars are sold (U.S. or another country), making the total cost part of U.S. production is simply an out and out lie. Greed and disingenuous distortion unfortunately seem to go together as a villainous combination. Such a combined outrage is too often excused as legitimate accounting "efficiency" instead of the absolute fraud it is.

Worse, all foreign cars assembled in the United States are included. This is also the case with all foreign brands of whatever products are simply put together here. (Remember, as well, that the profits of these companies go back to the foreign countries involved!)

Fourth, the kinds of new industries created do not, in most cases, require the same number of workers (nor many of the skills of laid-off workers) as a percentage of their output that the lost industries do. So, jobs are lost in that respect even if old industries are replaced by new ones. Remember the basic facts: *real* jobs (decent wages) = personal income = purchasing power = economic health. Fewer *real* jobs = lower income = less purchasing = economic problems.

Fifth, the education and skills needed for these new industries are more advanced than those needed for the old industries, and the number of jobs are far fewer. So, in both respects , limited opportunities are afforded to workers displaced by the loss of old industries. In short, the number of jobs generated by new industries is insufficient to provide enough jobs for the people who are unemployed as a result of the loss of old industries— even if their skills qualified them which generally they don't.

Most appalling, and dangerous, is that former job-holders in outsourced industries (unemployed and underemployed) seem, in many quarters, just to be written off—doomed never to work again!

Sixth, the number of jobs required at this time in the country's history to prevent substantial unemployment is greatly expanded by the dramatic increase in population from both natural growth and legal immigration—an increase far greater than that seen a decade—much less several decades—ago.

In the final analysis, we no longer produce many of the products we need for our own use—consumer products such as shoes, apparel, furniture, appliances, home furnishings, and other manufactured products, not to mention many foodstuffs and drugs and so on ad nauseam. Even more critical, we don't have adequate domestic steel supplies and many other vital materials for the defense of this nation. The car situation is an issue unto itself and an even greater economic disaster.

As mentioned earlier, in too many "production" figures, our financial "products"—sold here and across the world—are included. Since this part of our economic activity has dominated the country's business life and "success," as well as playing a big role in many of the "production" and "export" numbers (GDP and GNP), one has to wonder what will take their place, assuming the current crisis is overcome. In other words, what will replace the gigantic hole in economic "production" caused by this blow-out? If it's not a return of the old manufacturing base, our future is in serious question, not to say desperate straits! Such a dire prediction is both for *real* jobs and for the literal defense of this nation. We need a combination of the new technology industries *and* the old basic industries if we are to have *real* jobs once more in this country, again assuming we are able to overcome the current (2009) economic catastrophe.

It is also of course true that our exports depend upon the economic health of nations that buy our products. However, the health of the U.S. economy is vital to them as well for their exports. So, isn't this the typical chicken and egg situation? Yes, in a way it is. Nevertheless, the chicken has to be healthy to lay edible eggs in order for them to be bought. In other words, both the producer and the buyer have to be in good economic health for their trade to prosper.

Consequently, what is required to make international trade work to advantage for all concerned is truly *fair* trade. It can not be "free" trade where one country, such as China, has an unfair advantage because of cheap labor rates, a lack of pollution control requirements, inordinate subsidies, and on and on!

We should import on fair terms from China certain products that they can produce better than we can, and they similarly from us. However, one-way trade based on unfair factors is bad for both parties. A reasonable balance based on fair conditions should be helpful to each party. The result almost certainly would be a substantial reduction of Chinese imports to the United States and a large increase in U.S. exports to China—but based on a rational and fair formula for international trade. The reduction in China's exports to the United States could be balanced by using that capacity for exports to other countries or consumption in China's own growing domestic market.

From a policy standpoint the United States is undoubtedly and understandably leery of China's reaction because of the amount of U.S. debt held by China. What China needs to realize, however, is that its interests will be far better served by a healthy world overall where it can sell its products to many countries, rather than having too many of its eggs in one basket—the United States. This means that for such a situation to exist in the world, the U.S. economy—as said many times, still the world's single largest market by far—must be healthy. The United States has to be a consuming market for the world to prosper. Clearly, though, our country needs a better balance of its export/import trade not only for its own interests but also for those of the world at large.

The health of the U.S. economy can be revived only by the return of *real* jobs to the middle class of this country. In the view of this writer, that objective can best be achieved by the Equalization Formula that is addressed in the section immediately below and also later in this book. Other means are examined, but this one (while undoubtedly facing the most difficult political obstacles) holds the greatest promise. It is explained in what follows and briefly described in the letter to William Ford that can be found in Appendix 1 of this book.

By the way, it is useful to note again what countries' economies are growing at the most rapid rates. They are China and India by far—and the growth rates for both are based on manufacturing increases.

Basis of the Equalization Formula

The Equalization Formula envisioned here applies to all industries. It covers every part, component, sub-assembly, assembly, finished product, and process or intellectual property produced outside of the United States and brought into this country for sale here. Whether the company involved is foreign or American makes no difference. The Formula applies equally to both—for anything produced or assembled outside of this country and sold here. In the case of foreign plants in the United States only imported elements would be subject to the Equalization Formula. Foreign companies that produce in the United States and also bring in finished products would have all those finished imported products covered by the Formula too.

The Formula would vary from country to country where any such "product" is either manufactured or put together. The calculation would be based on the difference between the cost of production in the producing country and that in the United States. The factors to be taken into consideration would include such things as average cost of labor (slave, prison, or otherwise); subsidies; deliberate exchange rate distortions; pollution requirements; laws necessitating expenditures, such as fire protection and safety measures; tax levies; union membership; pension, health, and other benefits; as well as any other cost-of-production variables in comparison with reasonable, fair amounts for U.S. costs.

These cost differentials, plus foreign government subsidies for production and/or export or both, should constitute the basis for this formula, the result of which would be a consolidated percentage for each specific product classification. The percentage ought to be levied by the United States on the price of the product to the U.S. buyer (intra-company transfers by American companies being subject to the same treatment). A tariff? Of course! But it's truly a *fair* one based on the rational equalization of trade, not rapacious "free" trade that has proven to be anything but for the workforce and middle class of this nation.

Important, too, is that the producing country's technological advances in product or production techniques are not to be included. So, cost advantages from such developments made through innovational and entrepreneurial resources could be fully realized in the pricing of a product—thus giving the originating country an advantage based on its own ingenuity.

If the objective of "free" trade was to make large fortunes for a relatively few "captains of the world," it was a great success.

Simply check the lists of millionaires and billionaires in this country and correlate the dates on which they made their money with the annual volume of imports passing through this country's ports, airports, and electronic money transfers. Also, check the number of *real* job losses during these years. In addition, correlate "financial products" totals and sub-totals for exports and domestic consumption if you can find these figures. Good luck!

To get the *real* job loss numbers for products (even without including "financial" products) requires more than just finding the figures for the outsourcing of jobs and the insourcing of cheap foreign labor to replace American workers. Also needed is an extrapolation for the billions of dollars of imports in terms of millions of American jobs that could have been available had those imports been produced in this country. (Good luck again in trying to get these numbers too! The ones published are not exactly iron clad. Others don't even exist. Regardless, the point is only too obvious without an erstwhile Einstein's help aided by Houdini.)

When checking the correlations, look particularly at top executives on Wall Street, in the big banks, and in other financial organizations and corporations (especially "global" corporations). Also, when considering financial interests, try correlating specifically financial exports (e.g., bundled mortgages, etc.) and electronic money imports. This subject opens a whole different can of worms. Realistically there is no possibility that such figures (at least valid ones) can be had. The pursuit of them unfortunately is an utter waste of time.

Back to the fundamental subject, however, the Equalization Formula. The following inclusion for *fair* trade would be the cause of an even greater firestorm, but from different quarters. Ideally, the Formula would also apply to all "products" made in the United States for sale here by U.S. facilities of foreign companies, and not just to imported parts, components, or final products. The automobile industry is an obvious case in point—the most evident—but there are others. However, this inclusion might be foregone to save infinite difficulties for our overseas operations.

In many instances, foreign car companies (and other foreign enterprises as well) both import parts and components from their home country (other, as well) and manufacture or buy parts and components here too—primarily assembling vehicles made from both imported and U.S.–produced parts. They have established such production capabilities in the United States for a variety of reasons. Not the least is protection against the day when the United States will awaken to the need for it to demand *fair* trade for imported products if the American Dream is to survive or even if there is to be an America we can recognize. Only what they import would be subject to the Equalization Formula.

Regardless of their shrewd and far-sighted vision, these foreign interests should not be allowed such an unfair competitive advantage, especially since their profits are returned to their home country. Because of many factors (one example being parts, components, assemblies, and final products imported after having been produced in other countries where manufacturing costs are lower than in the United States) there is a substantial cost differential. These foreign companies clearly have U.S. production at a major cost disadvantage. Additionally, American manufacturers have problems with union and non-union legacy issues, such as wages, pensions, and health benefits. They need to be adjusted on a rational basis. These issues are not new; they go back decades. In fairness, there have also been issues relating to quality and design, but such issues are for the most part things of the past.

However, American manufacturers' problems notwithstanding, there is, and has been for a long time, a crying need to give the domestic industries a fair shake. The U.S. Government (several administrations and congresses) has not had the vision or an understanding of the need for *fair* trade, much less of national self-preservation, to do this. The real question is why. Demolishing our manufacturing infrastructure and replacing it with a financial shell game is not exactly sound national policy, even on an irrational basis.

Equally incredible are the subsidies provided by various states in this country to foreign companies willing to locate in their jurisdictions. Sell out a basic U.S. industry in the long term for short-term political gain is the sorry reality! Yet, these states are only responding competitively to an incursion encouraged by the federal government at the expense of American industry. So, who is the real culprit?

Despite protestations of these foreign companies about jobs for Americans in their organizations and jobs and profits for American suppliers, such foreign companies' sales certainly afford them an unfair advantage because of the myriad reasons outlined here. For far too long our country has allowed these travesties of fairness, aided and abetted—but understandably—by those various states' tax breaks and their other incentives in one form or another. Little wonder that we find ourselves experiencing a financial disaster in addition to the ongoing loss of our critical manufacturing base. The facts are not new. In too many cases they have been hidden or covered up. In others, it seems, we have ignored the reality, didn't understand it or wouldn't (chose not to?) believe it for whatever reasons.

However, now it is long past the time when honesty should prevail over dishonest (but too often legal) greed in our country. The wails of these foreign enterprises, their lobbyists, many U.S. "global" corporations, Wall Street, and our governmental puppets should no longer be allowed to carry the day. (All of this should have been stopped years ago!) If things continue as they are, the final sell-out of our nation will have buried us.

No doubt the bleating about our foreign debts will be another issue. Nevertheless, consider what other countries are experiencing. The American economy is very sick. Therefore, other nations are very sick, because this market was essential for the health of their economies. With the U.S. recovery (soon to be hoped for but more likely not around the corner) will come the recovery of other nations. The United States will continue to be an important market for other countries (just not as relatively large as it once was) if we again have a major manufacturing base here. Would these other countries choose to cut their own throats for debt repayment? Unlikely! There are too many dangerous ramifications.

Could this formula be used in reverse against our exports? Quite possibly, at least in some cases where the host country is competing. Where not, probably not. In the former case, the likelihood would be dependent upon the need/desire for the product and volume required (for their own domestic market) above the host country's own production capacity, as well as various other possible economic and political considerations. The fundamental point is that the United States should restore its manufacturing base* for the

---

*It should be noted that, where this book talks about manufacturing, it means manufacturing for both old and new industries. The real difference is that old industries should be able to be re-started in far less time with existing technology and available markets. New industries generally will take longer, since many require new technology and new markets. Other new industries actually don't exist, even as ideas, because they haven't been conjured up yet (simply not born as the kernel of a thought in somebody's mind). The old industries can help solve the unemployment problem sooner. The new industries will help solve this problem in the longer term.

In any new industries we must prevent technology thefts or giveaways from government or the private sector as have occurred in the past (e.g., Internet from the Defense Department; computer, I believe, from NASA; automotive technology and production from Ford, General Motors, and Chrysler; and on and on). China actually *right now* makes a large percentage of our solar panels and wind turbines. With many U.S. corporations garnering approximately 46 percent of their profit abroad, how can they be kept in the U.S.? One way would be to use congressional legislation to shut them out of the U.S. market, were such a threat to arise, or to prevent them from selling or investing in U.S.

critical benefit of its own people, so that they can benefit from newly available jobs and in order for the country to regain the capability of making what is necessary for its own defense. It would do so if the Equalization Formula was instituted. If the Formula, or something like it, is not utilized, this nation's future will be in severe jeopardy!

If a formula like this is implemented, imports would be *fairly* available in what is still the world's single largest market and one, therefore, that foreign marketers would continue to covet but would now have to sell on an equitable basis. Exporters might moan and groan in certain instances for a while, at least until necessary adjustments were made to target other appropriate markets. The world would be better off, because competition would be more balanced and not dependent in too large part upon the economic climate of the world's largest consumer nation. Witness what is happening right now. U.S. consumer spending has dropped precipitously, and the whole world is hurt badly for loss of this market. It is not the only factor in the world's chaos by any means, but it certainly is a massive one.

Here is the foundation of the Equalization Formula. For easy figures, let's say that the total cost differential of producing a particular model of a foreign car (or a U.S. car) from all/some foreign components is $5,000 and the present price of the car to a dealer in the United States is $25,000; and that

---

markets directly or through any devious subterfuge. Does Congress have the courage and wisdom required? Unlikely! However, herculean pressure from us, the citizens, could make the difference.

Unfortunately, too many of our corporations view themselves as global and no longer U.S. entities. Nevertheless, the possibility of losing 54 percent of their profits should encourage them to have second thoughts. We should have no problem in finding replacements for those willing to take such a loss. However, a prospective corporate defector also would have to consider other substantial hits, such as asset losses, stock and capital effects, talent disaffection, etc.

this price then has a 20 percent equalization fee added to it. In such case, what the foreign manufacturer (or U.S. manufacturer producing outside the U.S. or inside the U.S. with foreign components) would probably do is add that $5,000 to the price of the car paid by the dealer, making it $30,000.

Thus, the price to the dealer would reflect the cost differential between foreign manufacture and true U.S. manufacture (all U.S. parts and assembly)—thereby equalizing the production cost between the two. A higher price to the U.S. buyer for this car? Yes, in all probability, or a far lower profit margin to the manufacturer (foreign or U.S.) or dealer. Is the foreign car (or U.S. car made from all/some foreign parts) price increase fair to the U.S. consumer? Many will say "of course not." However, the truth is quite the opposite; it is *fair* trade, not free trade. *That* means, jobs for Americans, income for Americans, a revival of the American Dream and an economic resuscitation for America! The alternative is a cheaper car. Which do we want? We can't have it both ways!

Free trade means killing U.S. jobs, destroying our manufacturing base, weakening our defense capability—among many other adverse effects—and ultimately major economic destruction. It also means slave labor, world pollution, building up the military strength of potential, if not present, enemies (through unfair profits and trade surpluses for foreign countries) and other negative results. *Fair* trade by way of cost equalization means just the opposite. Fair!

Manufacturers, foreign and U.S., must compete on a truly fair basis, or, in other words, the attributes of their products. No longer would foreign companies and masquerading American companies (American name but foreign product) be able to pirate the U.S. market on an unfair price basis which is the result of those lower costs for production from slave wages, no pollution controls, government subsidies, and so forth. All these evil and unfair practices plus numerous additional ones are mentioned more often than one might like but are critically important to keep in the front of our minds nonetheless. Hence the drum-beat!

An example of how the $5,000 cost differential is reached might be something like this. (Note that the percentage is totally theoretical—in actual fact, the figure might not be anything like 20 percent; it would depend upon the country of manufacture and the specific product.) For the sake of this example, what is presented is simply an outline—the numbers are pure figments of imagination. In a real application, arriving at the actual figures would require much digging and hard scrutiny. In this instance, the numbers used are for a single unit, one car. This example is merely for the purpose of illustrating how the Equalization Formula might be approached.

Price of foreign or U.S. (produced from foreign assembly/ components)	
manufacturer's car to dealer (original)	$25,000
Equalization fee = 20%	5,000
Price of car paid by dealer (actual)	$30,000

Composition of equalization fee (20%) is based on Equalization Formula for these hypothetical cost factor differentials (U.S. manufacturer's cost disadvantages with all U.S. parts and final product made in U.S.A.):

Labor rate	$ 1,500
Labor benefits (reasonable)	1,500
Pollution controls, etc.	1,000
Government subsidy	1,000
	$ 5,000*

---

*$5,000 = 20% of original foreign (or U.S.–produced from foreign components) manufacturer's $25,000 price to car dealer (or 20% equalization fee).

In short, without the Equalization Formula the foreign or U.S. (produced from foreign assembly/components) manufacturer has a 20 percent production cost advantage over true U.S. manufacturers, which gives the former an absolutely unfair advantage. It is utterly unjustifiable unless we are willing to sacrifice the American standard of living, and ultimately our very survival, for a lower price today that leads to disaster for our country tomorrow.* And this tomorrow is nearer than we may think—too close for even this generation, let alone those to follow! Our current economic disaster, as well as that being experienced throughout the rest of the world because of it, unfortunately gives clear evidence of this harsh and extremely dangerous reality. Do we want to re-claim America or trash it? Third World status is being forced upon most of us by our so-called leaders unless "Made in the U.S.A." brings back *real* jobs and our country from the abyss on whose edge we are teetering!

There are millions upon millions of Americans in the unemployment lines (with many more millions dependent upon them). These millions are those very people who in large part

---

*It is worth noting that some foreign manufactured goods, even with the Equalization Formula in effect, would rightly be sold in the U.S. market without application of the Formula. Rightly, because in certain cases particular products would or could not be produced in the U.S. (and never have been), since we are not able to offer the unique character, craftsmanship, or material involved in specific items such as Italian hand-crafted leather goods, Shetland Isles hand-loomed woolens, and so forth. In other words, these products (as contrasted with computer chips) are unique to their country of origin for whatever reason; they might be produced exclusively in a particular nation as a result of some local factor (e.g., hand-knitted Irish fishermen's sweaters) or may simply be indigenous to a particular part of the world (e.g., certain precious stones from Burma and others from Africa). Legitimate patented products would be treated similarly. However, any unique product might be subject to whatever tariffs apply when imported.

were essential to the nation's output when it was a highly successful manufacturing economy—by far the largest in the world—and not so terribly long ago. It should be again and can be, putting these millions back to work in a truly productive way. Remember when we were the world's leading creditor and not its largest debtor as we are now!

What is both appalling and unconscionable is that there are beginning to be heard (trial balloons?) among the so-called seers and savants commentaries about the unemployed simply being work force misfits for present-day economic opportunities. Therefore they are just to be written off.

The plaintive cry of the apologists is that regrettably many of the unemployed are disposable (although they are a significant percentage of the middle class), unfortunately obsolete factors of production (that is, manufacturing). A baleful excuse at best!

What is implied is that for a large percentage of the unemployed there are no jobs and won't be at any foreseeable time. There is clearly no place for these people in the visionaries' view of the nation's future. The unemployed can have no reasonable expectation of ever working again! Can you imagine actually eliminating several generations of workers?

"Certainly too bad, but technology has just passed them by," sayeth the hypocrites of greed. Truly holier-than-thou insincerity and an attempted cover-up for the inability of our government (Administration and Congress) to find and implement a workable solution for our country's desperate straits.

This write-off of people's lives defies belief and is abhorrent in every possible sense. The rationalization for such a sorry and sordid prospective policy is without doubt dereliction of the worst kind. Such a policy *must not* be allowed , or there will be absolutely no hope for our beloved United States of America! *Stop* such reprehensible and egregious action in any way necessary! *Stop it we absolutely must!*

PART TWO

Millions of Americans' Jobs
Raped
by America's So-called "Leaders"!

We Must Stop Them!

Original text as written in the early 1990s,
with later addenda in footnotes

FOREWORD

By Jane Waterhouse

The Setting: A typical American household.
The Time: One day not too far in the future.

    It's getting on towards dinner. Scott Barrett, age twelve, sits at his PC (manufactured in Japan) trying hard to finish his history homework. The deal is, if he gets it all done, his parents will let him play his new video game (also made in Japan) or maybe watch a video on the VCR (made in Germany) before they sit down to eat.

    Better hurry, he thinks. In the next room his mom is already setting out the placemats (made in China) and the plates (made in Taiwan) on the table (made in Sweden). The turkey is nuking in the microwave (manufactured in South Korea). He hears the clip-clop of his mom's shoes (made in "Yugoslavia") as she steps into the den. "What's doin', kiddo?"

    "Nothin' much," Scott tells her. "Only I could use some help with these history terms."

    Mom checks her watch (made in Switzerland). "Gee, d'ya think you could wait till your father gets back from work (at the American headquarters of a

Japanese company)? I've got to put together the fruit (grown in Mexico) salad."

Scott hears the sound of his dad's car (manufactured in Japan from an American design) pulling into the driveway. "Sure," he tells his mom. She leaves, heading back toward the custom (French) kitchen.

Mr. Barrett comes in, setting down his leather briefcase (made in Brazil); loosening his silk tie (made in Italy) and taking off his suit jacket (made in Great Britain). "Hey, Scott."

"Hey, Dad." Scott gives him a high-five. "Think you can help me with these definitions for my American history class?"

"I'll do what I can," his dad tells him. Scott knows he's being modest. His dad is a real ace when it comes to history.

"Here's one for you," Scott says, "The Industrial Age."

"Well son," Mr. Barrett tells him, "The Industrial Age took place in the United States from about the latter part of the nineteenth century to the latter part of the twentieth century. That's when most of the great mechanical inventions were made and the factory system got its start."

"Okay," says Scott, "now how about this American ingenuity?"

"American ingenuity," his father replies. "That's easy. It refers to how people all around the world regard us because of our creativity and inventiveness in the marketplace. They also respect and appreciate the great quality of 'Made in America' which that ingenuity represents."

"Run that by me again," Scott says, confused.

"Well, it's the spark that sets us apart, and enables us to make and do so many things," Mr. Barrett explains.

"Make things like what?" Scott wants to know.

"Like—," his father stammers, "—like…" His voice drifts off for a moment. When he picks up again, Mr. Barrett says, "Well, a long time ago, before you were born, we used to make…" And his voice becomes sad. Nostalgic almost.

Today's Forecast

You don't need radar and a weather map for today's forecast. All you have to do is look around. The storm is upon us! Foreign competition is forcing American industries out of business. In areas where the United States was once the inventor and world leader—areas such as consumer electronics and appliances and on and on—we're virtually out of business. Our basic industries are disappearing. Workers have been displaced and demoralized. Real unemployment and underemployment (partial employment) are high. Not only have we become a debtor nation for the first time in history, we've become the world's largest debtor at that.

The storm is no longer on the horizon. The clouds are twisters of death and destruction which have ripped into our cities and farmlands, leaving them ghost towns without industries and farms of eroding, arid land (or farms lost to families by corporate and foreign acquisition). This storm is shaking the foundations of corporate America's work force social contracts with gale force winds. Our very way of life is threatened. But this is no time to take to the cellar and wait things out. If we are to survive, we must stem the tides, and face them head-on, with our eyes open. Just as in the face of a natural disaster, when people band together to rebuild and start anew, so, too, in light of this potential national disaster we must take steps to battle the storm. We have to move away from the eye of this tornado in which there can only be a further downward spiral, and the eventual destruction of all we hold near and dear. And we must act now! The vortex of the tornado is descending upon us—wreaking devastation upon our country and bringing death to our very way of life. A volcano is waiting to erupt—pouring more devastation over our land and bringing death to all we cherish. Today's forecast is tomorrow's disaster! And act now we must or lose all that the American Dream means.

What does all this have to do with me?

The bad news is that good jobs are being lost in frightening numbers throughout our economy, particularly in manufacturing. This bad news doesn't take any special sort of insight to impart, or true genius to understand. It's all around us. Everywhere we look. We have two choices. We can close our eyes to what we see and pretend that it doesn't exist—until someday we are no longer able to pretend anymore, because it is too late. Or, we can do something about it.

And here's the good news. The good news is that this book offers a concrete, tangible, and sure way of creating positives from all these negatives. But these are big issues, the reader might object, more complex and deep-seated than any one person can tackle. Why, chairmen of international corporations...economists...our government's "statesmen"...and philosophers...haven't been able to extricate us from the mire in which we find ourselves! How then, can one individual make a difference?

The answer is that perhaps a few of the CEOs and "statesmen," the pragmatists and polemicists of our time, have not seen the connections stemming from the singular problem that has struck every aspect of American society. Because there's no doubt about it—one problem underlies all of the issues, critical issues facing us—and yet no one has chosen to identify it, much less address it. Too many deliberately avoid it. What? Loss of *good* jobs! Well, if all of these smart and educated people—these experts—haven't come to terms with it, the reader may well say "What makes you think I can?"

The answer is probably more evident than we might suspect, despite the enormity of this potential death-knell for our nation. It will be found by the approximately 260 million real experts finally getting the facts—the truth—for once. We're talking about the American people—you, me, the person who fixes your telephone, the woman who helped build your car, the teacher who instructs your children, the people who collect your garbage—individuals throughout our once great nation. The smartest person in the world can't make the right decision with the wrong information, barring a miracle!

The basic fact is that we are not permitted to know the truth unless we are faced with such truth—in this case, sadly and all too often, by being numbered among its casualties. Then, the hard-rock reality is inescapable. "Few facts," too often misrepresentations, lead to grave doubts. The government tells us it has created millions of jobs without letting us know how many millions have been lost, how much the lost jobs paid, and how little the new ones do. Two, three or four jobs to earn a family's survival is hardly job "creation"! And it is not exactly a living, much less living the American Dream!

Until now, the end result has been a massive—and just about universal—sense of hopelessness among the one-third of our work force that has been hit and hurt, a despair of ever being able to effect change. Everywhere we're surrounded by the specters of apathy and debilitation or, even worse, the sort of helpless anger that leads to the tearing down, or dropping out, of the society in which we live.

"Okay," you say. "But again—what does all this have to do with me?"

The answer is "everything," especially if you recognize yourself in one or more of the following situations or similar ones. Everyone needs to know the realities for a reasonable assessment of their situation. Then, that assessment must be heard in order to count. The question, at this point, is "how to make being heard happen."

Is this you or someone you know?
- You're aware of current events, and you are a person who has seen the danger in what is happening to the U.S. job market!
- You listen carefully, and you are a person who suspects the truth about the nature of the vaunted government claims for the U.S. job

market! ("Things are not always what they seem; milk often masquerades as cream.")

- Your boss pulls you aside and asks for your opinion. You find yourself tempering your words, holding back. When he walks away, you're sure he's thinking he's gotten a good picture of the way things are going. But you know what he really got was a watered-down version of the truth. He doesn't want the facts unless they help to improve his promotion possibilities. (When he wants *your opinion*, he'll *tell you* what it is!)

- You are the boss. You walk into a work station. Conversation stops. You ask your employees about a new work practice. One person speaks up, offering something noncommittal, and the others either nod or say nothing. You guess that means it's going well. But are you sure you've gotten the whole story? Not likely in that corporate culture!

- It's Monday afternoon, the weekly meeting again. It's pretty much a waste of time, but the boss thinks it's valuable. You'll go in, as usual, and tell her exactly what she wants to hear. That's how you survive!

- Here comes another manufacturing productivity group. Afterward, everyone will make the proper noises about just how helpful and incisive it was, but deep down everybody recognizes that they've only dealt with the fluff, with the obvious. The really controversial issues remain well hidden in the corporate closet. Understandably—people don't want their jobs moved to Indonesia!

- It's Friday, 4:45 PM, only fifteen more minutes to the week-end. Your life here at work is a drudgery. Most of the time you just feel like a robot, a human machine. You can't remember the last time anyone asked for your opinion, or you went home satisfied in the fact that you'd made some sort of worthwhile contribution. Not that you didn't have plenty of ideas on how your area could be improved and work more effectively. Oh, well, you'll have to get your satisfaction on Saturdays and Sundays. Monday through Friday you're just chalking up that time until retirement—praying that you're not going to be a victim of "right-sizing" or the "Asian Tigers" (China, India, Taiwan, Korea—you name it)!

- You're the new person. You walk into the executive dining room, and for a moment the conversation sputters out. You can feel all eyes on you. A split second later people are talking in overloud voices about anything but business. "What's the matter," you joke to your companion, "do they think I'm a corporate spy or something?" When he answers, he isn't smiling. "You hit the nail on the head," he replies. "It's common knowledge that management uses them!"

- You were hired because of your creativity, but with every project it's been stifled more and more. Now, instead of presenting your best ideas, you just offer the ones they're most likely to go with. You know the business will end up suffering because so much great stuff never sees the light of day, but you're tired of beating your head against a wall. Give 'em what they want, right? Right—unless you want to be a thinker without a job!

- Your co-worker approaches you quietly at the water cooler. "I need to talk to you," she says, "but I can't afford for the boss to see us together. Can we meet for dinner?" You can't afford to have the boss see you at the water cooler with her either!

- You were denied that last promotion for being outspoken. You were denied such a promotion for going above and beyond the call of your duties. Your boss thought you were competing for his job—particularly since you are a capable young woman.

- You've just been laid off. They said they were overstaffed. You didn't have seniority, so you had to go—even though your last review called you "a valuable asset to the company." You notice that the man who hired you is still here. In fact, no one from upper management—those who presumably are responsible for this bloated situation—is being let go. Worse, you were hired less than a year ago!

- Today is your last day. You've been a secretary with this company for thirty-four years, but now that your boss is retired they're saying there is no job for you. They gave you a party at lunch, and presented you with a watch, wishing you good luck in your future ventures. What future ventures, you wonder? At fifty something it won't be easy to find another position. When were you joined at the hip with your boss, you wonder again? More frightening, fifty isn't old, but it's too old to get a comparable job without a miracle happening. Actually, forty is probably considered "over the hill."

- You notice one of your co-workers cleaning out her desk. "What happened to her?" you ask a colleague. "She made a mistake," he says, "she told the truth!"

If you are any of these people or identify with their situations or similar ones, you already might be a victim or could be at any time. Rational people are not irrational. Yet, they often function irrationally if they do not have the facts for rational assessments and decisions. The people here, in some cases, probably were denied the facts, or they themselves chose to deny them for whatever reasons. Regardless, they were prospective victims or actual ones.

These are organizational examples with which we are all too familiar. They typify what has happened to the jobs in our country. We have been blindsided, or we chose to be blind (for our own reasons). It doesn't matter. The mission here is to remove the blinders, take a good hard look at the jobs disaster, and consider some serious alternatives.

The message of this book is that we can stop the plunder—but only if we act quickly!

PREFACE

You've picked up this little book. Maybe you were intrigued by its title. Maybe something about the cover attracted you, or perhaps it simply caught your eye because it was in one of your favorite sections of the store. But how do you know it's for you?

Well, that's simple. You should read this book if you are discontented, frustrated, or disillusioned with your job or if, worse still, you have lost your job or feel you may lose it. This is a book for people with high management...middle management...lower management...and no management jobs: the guy on the assembly line, the woman who's just started her own business, the nearly retired factory worker, and the about-to-be college graduate can all find something that pertains directly to them on these pages.

Oh, and by the way, if you're concerned at the state of things around you—too high unemployment (despite contrary government "statistics"), too low *true* productivity, working two or three jobs combined that pay less than your previous one, millions of jobs lost by Americans to slave or cheap labor in other countries, the decline of industry, the encroachment of foreign competition—there's something important in this book for you. Are you at a personal crossroads? At a loss about what to do next? Help is to be found here, so read on.

Finally, if you're an American who is perplexed and frightened by the economic situation—if you had it better in the past, and you want to know what happened, or if you want a better future for yourself, your children, your friends, your country—turn these pages, because there is help, and there is hope. There is a workable solution.

Just identifying the issues is an important step toward that solution. Whether or not you agree with all, some, or none of the corrective actions suggested isn't the point of this book. On the contrary, my goal is simply to raise issues for your deliberation and action, or not, as you see fit. If you agree in whole or part with even one suggestion, all the better. If you agree with nothing more than that even one of the issues, some, or all deserve your attention (and you believe solutions are possible), then this book will be worthwhile for you.

Much of what you will read here is based upon our own experiences and those of other people whose views we value greatly. Many of these experiences go back to World War II. Others originated with the beginning of the Reagan years in the White House. Some are as recent as right now. No punches are pulled.

Since the book is intended to be short, there is no exhaustive back-up data. Nevertheless, it can obviously be had elsewhere, if anyone so desires, for issues that involve data (some valid; unfortunately some not; too much simply non-existent). It cannot be had for other issues that don't involve data and are derived from experience and observation. On the other hand, there are more than enough hard facts (data) in chapter 7 to make the statistical case unequivocally.

We are being, and have been, disastrously led astray for a long time not only about jobs but also about what is being done to us and our once great country. We must somehow stop this destruction of our lives and dreams. This book will try to enlist your participation in the critical battle to bring back the American Dream for Americans and for all people to whom the American Dream is a life-giving aspiration.

INTRODUCTION

This book is for all Americans who have lost their jobs or are in danger of losing them—unskilled, semi-skilled, skilled, supervisory or managerial jobs. And who isn't, as this country exists today? Very few people, if any!

It is also for Americans who care about such things and care about this nation…and are scared. Remember, once—and not so very long ago—it was the home of the American Dream. Losing jobs is a disaster for the people involved and for our country as well. However, these disasters are swept under the rug by those who cause them. Isn't it strange that the people who make the decisions leading to such dire straits are *never* thrown to the wolves? Instead, it's always the people who work for them!

Decision-makers' rationalizations for such callousness and avarice are virtually without limit. "Our economy is strong, and this is simply the price we have to pay." Yes, it is strong for money manipulators and the like on Wall Street, as well as their minions in the corporate world and elsewhere. However, the jobs being lost are not theirs but yours and mine.

These manipulators are a basic cause of our job problems because of their demands on companies for ever greater profits, "the bottom line"—not a year or two from now but yesterday, today, or tomorrow at the latest. What quicker way to higher profits than lower costs—meaning fewer jobs! Fewer jobs at home that is, replaced by slave labor jobs in other countries. Unfortunately, such sordid excuses for human beings are not alone in their greed and cupidity, as will be discussed shortly. They have equally rotten collaborators in many—and in shockingly "high"—places.

Another of their rationalizations is even more absurd. "We must reduce jobs to compete in the world market." The truth is that the first thing we need to do is compete in the American market by making here in America many, many more of the products that are bought by Americans. Although the U.S. Congress could have acted (using, for example, positive and negative incentive plans) to preclude the real differential costs some U.S. companies confronted and could not counter otherwise, Congress did absolutely nothing. Instead, it championed "free" trade, choosing not to distinguish between "fair" and "free"!

The United States is far and away the world's single largest consuming market. And our so-called "leaders" have literally sold it, in one way or another and a massive degree, to many foreign pressure groups (companies and countries). This situation applies no less to innumerable U.S. "global" corporations and U.S. import companies. Such foreign enterprises and domestic importers (including many American corporations that once produced here and continue to use American brand names) wanted this whole mouth-watering pie, not just a fair piece of it. In short, these "leaders" have sold out the United States and sold our jobs down the river (over the border and beyond the seas) in the process.

This book is not a Washington "intellectual's" or "economist's" think-tank study. Neither is it an elitist "professor's" paper for an academic journal. Quite the opposite, it is the result of a seventeen-year effort to get our various elected administrations and congresses in Washington, during that time, to understand the inevitability of the developing jobs catastrophe and to do something about it.

Clearly, we were and have been engaged in an exercise of futility from the very start. The simple fact of this tragic fiasco is that they didn't want to understand it, because understanding it would have required questioning their own motivations and actions.

The disappearing jobs are Americans' jobs that have been sold out by our "leaders," who have actually moved them out of our country (offshore) to the lowest foreign bidders. This incredible dereliction is in addition to selling enormous pieces of the American market (companies, facilities, and other assets in addition to enormous chunks of the U.S. market for myriad products) to foreign interests.

The whole situation is a sorry and soul-searing commentary about how such people, along with our corporate chiefs, financial moguls, union heads, the media, and others have denied or—worse still—ignored the inevitability of the growing jobs problem for these many years (and more). They still deny that there is an issue, despite the critical nature of the situation. However, they have discovered that there is lots of media opportunity for their own selfish agendas in denying the existence of such a problem or minimizing it with fatuous ideas.

And still they offer no actual plans or real courses of action. Instead they offer rather theory, faulted statistics, lies, damned lies, drivel, and worse. The time has come (long since) to get the cards on the table and to *demand* very specific actions that will turn this jobs disaster around! Such actions are concrete and achievable, as spelled out in chapters 4 and 8. However, they do not include the absurd fantasies of the plunderers' mouthpieces. In short, no more utterly ludicrous and unconscionable programs and actions! No more re-training for jobs that don't exist! No more re-training for people who couldn't get the jobs even if they did get training—because they are too old, have too questionable a record, and on and on! No more downsizing for competitiveness in the stock market! No more selling our jobs to the lowest foreign bidders for global competitiveness (and Americans be damned)! No more selling the American market (and American jobs) to foreign interests (and once old-line American companies that produce abroad for cheap labor and other cost advantages but still use well-known American brand names). They tout the supposed consumer price advantage (hardly an advantage for Americans without jobs)!

Our seventeen-year effort with Washington for a *real* jobs plan obviously has fallen on *not just deaf ears but blocked minds* with their own self-serving purposes. Time has run out if our country is once again going to have good jobs for its people and prosper as before on a broad basis, not a limited one for an extremely small percentage called the "fortunate." The latter course can lead only to chaos. Now we Americans have to turn the tables and get our jobs back. We can do it if we pull together with a concerted effort and have a specific plan of action. The "leaders" who ignore us must know that they do so at their own grave peril. This book has its focus in sane capitalism, not the insane greed too often in clear view with myriad so-called "leaders."

America works for Americans when American workers work. It doesn't when they don't!

Note: We presented a draft letter to a leading business editor some time ago. The letter was simply a request that the present administration announce job losses from downsizing, mergers, and so forth, along with its periodic "job creation" figures. It was also suggested that the average pay of lost jobs and that of new jobs be included so that comparisons could be made and the realities seen. The letter contained several other similar proposals.

The editor's response was, "I agree with everything you say. However, nobody will publish it!" He strongly stated that what we were proposing would step on the toes of "leaders" who control the media (including newspaper, magazine, and book publishers) who don't want to have the American people aware of the truth. Why? Because any hue and cry from the people could unhorse these so-called "leaders" and put an end to their ill-gotten gains. Interesting? Damning and frightening!

This was an appalling indictment of what is supposedly a free press that constantly demands the right of free speech under the First Amendment.

However, the "free press" too often appears to prohibit "free speech" for anyone else if such views don't conform with those of the "free press" controllers and policymakers or follow the deceptions of their red herrings.

CHAPTER 1

THE JOBS DISASTER

Is it too late? Yes, for some!

"Hell is truth recognized too late." So, spoke Thomas Hobbes, the seventeenth-century philosopher. Sadly, and unbelievably, for many people who have already lost their very livelihoods, it is too late! Incredible to all of us has to be the fact that the people about whom we're talking are other Americans, if not actually ourselves. Many of them are our friends and neighbors.

They, and their families, "live" in this land of once great opportunity. Their futures have been destroyed as we watch their jobs disappear and the very foundation of our country undermined with promises of re-training for jobs that, at best, are pipe-dreams and, at worst, bald-faced lies.

All of this goes on as Wall Street plays the numbers game and the enormous fortunes of those relative few are compounded at a frightening rate.

But not all—yet!

Others of us may not be quite at that point of being a lost cause—yet! Nevertheless, if we don't quickly turn around the situation confronting us, we will be.

In this instance soon is late, because the issues have plagued us for many years. In some cases, nothing has been done about the problem; in others, the wrong thing has been done. So, time is truly of the essence. We must act now!

Who are the blackguards? Surprise!

Most of the ideas for dealing with these issues are detested by a relatively small group of Americans. They are the ones who are destroying our nation and the American Dream. While causing such devastation, they hide behind the charade they euphemistically call the "new global economy." What they really mean is jobs for any country where slave wages are lowest, but God forbid hiring Americans.

These same people live off America's bounty and our backs. Who are they? Surprisingly, many of them are so-called leaders in government, Wall Street, banking, business, the media, and universities as well as various other people who have important and powerful positions (many completely unknown) within our country. Some are citizens of other countries with similar greedy interests, roles, and values.

Worse still, it is these very people who actively connive at sending our jobs abroad—or, more accurately, selling our jobs—for their own personal gain. In too many cases the goal of such avarice is to reach growth and profit targets as a means of job and bonus retention at any cost—including the sacrifice of your and my jobs on the altar of their unspeakable gluttony. Such a problem unfortunately too often exists from the top through other levels in untold numbers of organizations. There are also those who engineer leveraged buyouts of great American companies with the result that long-time employees are thrown out into the street with no possibility of getting another *real* job in their lifetime. As you probably know, a leveraged buyout is usually a polite term for stealing a company. Unfortunately, there are also other terms for this, such as merger, acquisition and reorganization. Such buyouts are often paid for from the sale of the "bought" company's own assets, its available cash, or other less than salutary means, such as cost-cutting by moving manufacturing operations out of this country.

Why do they sell out this great country of ours?
For money and/or power!

For these sordid, rotten activities such people take home unconscionable amounts of money, legal and illegal. If you think baseball players make a lot of money, it's peanuts in this league! How about a few million to 30 million a year—or 100 million or who knows what? For some, power and status are their great rewards—even more than money. As Lord Acton said: "Power corrupts. Absolute power corrupts absolutely." This kind of power may not be absolute, but it's close enough to do absolute damage.

Are these issues critical?
Yes and worse! But they are fixable.

The issues in this book are tragically real—not theoretical or academic. They drastically affect you and me, our children, grandchildren, and generations beyond. These issues exist right now. They are hurting us badly at this very moment.

However, they will become disastrous for all of us in a short time if we allow them to persist. For many they already are disastrous; for others they have been for a long time. Despite all this, the tables can be turned if we face, and make known, the realities and deal with them now. At this time they are truly earth-shattering dangers to our economic and social ways of life and soon will be to our very existence if nothing is done. The job losses in this country are a present, and even worse, prospective disaster, because the implications of not making a major outcry about the sources for much of what we buy are basic and far reaching in many respects—to our jobs, to our economy, and literally to the actual defense of our nation.

We cannot continue to buy products from sources with cheap labor supplies and other unfair, often unconscionable cost advantages—and all at the expense of American jobs. The supposed justification for this rapacious destruction of the U.S. manufacturing base by those reaping the ill-gotten profits is premised on a totally invalid argument. Their contention is that "free" means "fair." It is no such thing—in fact, anything but!

"Free," as they use it, simply means the lowest price possible which, translated, means the highest profit for them. These sponsors of destruction for the U.S. manufacturing base and its good jobs unceasingly beat the drum for the free market or, as they try to rationalize it, the "global market." Such people have not the least concern for the elimination of American jobs or the disastrous loss it causes for millions of Americans and their families, much less the welfare of the nation itself. No, their greed for money and its power prevails above all else.

The simple truth, however, is that there is nothing fair in the clamorous cry of these avaricious predators for free trade. The rapacity of these people can be seen only too clearly in the subterfuges and deceits practiced by their foreign production sources, their foreign and domestic collaborators, and themselves.

Is this a war? Yes! And we must win it or see the defeat of our country!

We Americans are treated as mindless and willful children by too many "leaders" in our government and by other so-called leaders on Wall Street, in banks, and in other financial organizations, the media, business, universities and elsewhere, not to mention foreign influences.

Do these people realize what they are doing and do they care? The answer to the first question is that in most cases they know only too well. With regard to the second question, they care greatly— but only for their own rotten self-interests, not for you, me, and all those subjected to their evil depredations. Again, not true of all but far too many! There are, of course, exceptions to the culprits in the various influential areas of our society. Unfortunately, there just aren't nearly enough of these "good guy" fighters, with the vitally necessary clout, who have been brought to the party. It is critical that they be identified and enlisted in this effort.

The strategy of so many of our so-called leaders is endlessly to subject us to their unfortunately highly effective out-and-out propaganda. We must stop them from doing this by simply stopping them—period!

CHAPTER 2

REAL JOBS?
NOT UNLESS YOU BELIEVE IN LEPRECHAUNS
AND THE TOOTH FAIRY!
RE-TRAINING FOR NON-EXISTENT JOBS?
NO LESS DELUSIONAL!

What's at stake?

The basic heart and soul of our country, not to mention the engine that drives it, are at stake in this situation. These are the highest and most critical stakes imaginable! In a word, survival! What could be higher? Obviously nothing in this world!

That survival is dependent upon jobs, *real* jobs that involve making things—not temporary, part-time or low-paying service jobs in restaurants, health care facilities, fast-food establishments, and so on. *Real* jobs and real income are fundamental for a return to what used to be the American standard of living. They are also essential for a revival of families, their values, educational proficiency, an equitable society, and a civilized culture. Plus, they are necessary for effective attacks on crime, drugs, hunger, home-lessness, and the myriad other afflictions besetting us—not to mention our ability to defend ourselves as a nation. Otherwise, no American Dream! In fact, probably no America as we know it!

Who needs jobs?

The people in this country who are in the greatest need of jobs are unskilled, semi-skilled, and many categories of skilled workers along with lower and middle-level management employees. Many of these women and men are out of work altogether or are working in jobs that pay far less than they made in their previous jobs, having to take such low-paying work (sometimes several jobs) out of sheer desperation. Too often there is also the need to retain at least a small part of their self-respect by working at something.

Within these unemployed, "disemployed," and underemployed groups, think about the over-fifty woman or man, the teenage girl or boy, the high-school dropout, someone unable to read or write, a woman or man with a criminal record who has been rehabilitated, individuals who are the objects of ethnic and racial biases, and on and on. What chance do these people actually have for a *real* job in this country of ours as it exists today? Practically none if the truth be told!

This truth unfortunately just doesn't exist in governmental pronouncements, official statistics, and political out-and-out prevarications. One might ask why the media doesn't put out some of these facts. The answer has to be that they believe what they're told. They don't know the difference; they lie; they are controlled; or some combination of any or all.

Why are people who need real jobs not able to get them?

People in this country can't get jobs that don't exist in this country. Too many of the "leaders" (most!) won't do what's necessary to keep our jobs here or get them back, because these predators can profit more by plundering American jobs and selling them to the lowest bidder outside this country.

Why is it that such jobs do not exist?

The jobs we need do not exist for six basic reasons:

- First, after World War II we (America) rebuilt other countries' (most important, the countries of our former enemies) capabilities to compete with us, but not our own U.S. manufacturing base.
- Second, we gave these countries free rein to "borrow" our technologies following that war.
- Third, in the last thirty to thirty-five years we have permitted these and other countries to steal our industries and markets through a combination of stupidity, greed on the part of far too many "leaders," ludicrous trade agreements, absurd import regulations, and "slave" labor rates in various countries.
- Fourth, we have allowed many of our remaining manufacturers to "sell" American jobs abroad on their contention that they have no other way to compete in our own markets. (In a sense, they were right, because our import regulations and subsidies were less than adequate. However, these manufacturers and the

unions made dubious efforts at best to rectify the situation. Nevertheless, a few—a very few—have stood tall.

- Fifth, too many investors have encouraged American companies to show the "bottom line" desired by Wall Street overnight, through becoming "lean and mean." Translated, that means "dump" employees, since it's the easiest way to a quick profit. "The people, the company long term and the future of our nation be damned! Save the golden handshake and/or golden parachute for us, the management, any way we can." *Financial control (in fact, control overall) of our country has been ceded to Wall Street and its cohorts!*

- Sixth, we have not stopped foreign influences from "lobbying" our governmental bodies at the levels necessary for them to get legislation and rulings favorable to their interests in acquiring our industries, our companies, our markets, our jobs, a substantial part of our government (national debt)—in essence, our very substance. Even our country's basic defense is in certain aspects dependent on foreign countries as a result.

Is our situation hopeless?
Yes—if we accept the plunderers!
But we must not and need not.

It is worth noting again that the American market for practically anything is the single largest in the world by far—bigger than most of European countries combined. Therefore, American manufacturers should protect their sales (and jobs) in this market at virtually any cost. But too many have not—especially preferring instead the "global" market for jobs. What this means is producing any and everything cheaply abroad for sale back in the United States as supposedly American brands, thereby gaining large profits at the expense of American jobs. In other cases, foreign components and/or assemblies are brought into the American market and assembled here to gain more profits.

In still others (and too many) instances, importers bring in foreign products for retailers or retailers do it for themselves (for example, Wal-Mart brings in Chinese products). These products often bear a brand name that sounds American or maybe the brand actually is American (a company that was once an American manufacturer but now is really an importer). The possibilities for making these products seem what they are not (that is, American)—imported largely (but not all) from Asian countries—are virtually limitless. Even if the buyer knows the difference, the inexpensive price almost invariably wins the sale, particularly since no real American product is to be had.

How can this destruction of American jobs be stopped or significantly reduced? U.S. legislation should control the hemorrhaging of American jobs through a plan of negative and positive incentives (see chapters 4 and 8).* Why has such legislation

---

*There is also a Fair Trade Equalization Formula that has further advantages but is more complicated. It is presented in Pre-script 2010 of this book, as well as in Appendix 1, which contains a copy of a letter sent to Mr. William Clay Ford, Sr. of Ford Motor Company.

not been proposed and passed? Basically because it requires vision, courage, and true concern for America and its people—qualities that seem sadly in very short supply.

The legislative culprits (aided and abetted by their corporate cohorts) hide their infamy behind the façade of "free"—forget *fair*—trade and the blithe excuse of what they like to call the entrepreneurial spirit of capitalism. What a charade, disgrace, and egregious miscarriage of their duty to our nation now and to its future! This guilt is shared by many past congresses, as well as the current one. So, too, numerous administrations have been equally remiss for not having submitted, much less pushed, such legislation. An outrage, crime, and shame—all inflicted on people who elected these "leaders" and trusted them to protect the country's best interests and its well-being!

Could just one major industry make a difference? Yes. And what a difference!

As an example, let's accept a generally bandied about statement that one in eight American jobs is dependent upon the automotive industry either directly or indirectly. If total employment in this country is 130 million, roughly 16 plus million people have jobs dependent upon that industry. These jobs are in not just automotive manufacturing but in sales (dealerships), parts, and materials as well—such things as glass, steel, tires, plastics, batteries, fabrics, leather, and so forth (that is, the few U.S. companies remaining in each—but most being distributors and retailers, not manufacturers).

Supposedly, about 30 percent of the cars and trucks now sold in our country are foreign-made (some with U.S. assembly). When the actual percentages of foreign components in American cars and the foreign assembly of our cars are taken into account, the total is obviously far higher. However, this figure apparently is not available, simply because the people involved don't want us to know how great it really is. So, we'll stick with the 30 percent for now.

If the 30 percent were reduced to 15 percent, our country would recover about 2.5 million full-time *real* jobs, manufacturing jobs, and obviously many others as well—not just temporary or part-time or low-pay service jobs. That's a large number of *real* jobs, and from only one industry. In addition, there would still be plenty of foreign cars sold here every year; 15 percent of the American market is a lot of cars (2,000,000–2,500,000).

What is needed to make the difference?

To make this change back to American jobs first (not for just cars but for all product categories involved), we need courage, vision, and *patriotism* primarily among government, manufacturers and unions—and the financial community too. They would have to put together a plan of incentives for American buyers of American products, a plan of disincentives for American manufacturers who sell our jobs abroad, and a plan of penalties for American importers of foreign manufactured goods, importers who bring these goods to the American market and put an American label on them even though the products are in large part or totally not American at all. The plan would need in some way to address at least one of these incentives, disincentives, or penalties but preferably all of them if we want to put American jobs first again. And we must. GATT (the General Agreement on Tariffs and Trade), the "World Trade Agreement," and NAFTA (North American Free Trade Agreement) or any other such trade arrangement cannot be allowed to stand in the way.

"Free markets?" A tragic joke!

Free markets don't exist for the countries and companies that take advantage of America. In other words, it doesn't go both ways. They don't return such foolish generosity, because they know it's self-destructive. Unfortunately, "we" have not yet understood this reality.

They also know that we have been "naive" enough to permit this one-sided economic slaughter (with its incredible job losses), because our self-serving, greedy "leaders," the plunderers, have proclaimed something they euphemistically call the "global economy" that demands such sacrifice—ours, of course, not theirs. So far, we have let them get away with it. "They" must be stopped—now! Or there will be little, if anything, left for America to offer in the way of *real* jobs, much less the once vaunted American standard of living.

We have to remember that the "they" are also our leaders, the plunderers in government, politics, Wall Street, banking, corporations, media, academia, and in other areas, though these are the foremost culprits. As such, they are the ones who are selling our American jobs, in one way or another, to the lowest bidder in foreign countries and our American market (we apologize for saying it again—far and away the world's single largest) to foreign producers. These plunderers are too often supposedly American companies, as mentioned before, selling products under American names (frequently long-time, well-known household brands), products manufactured in other countries with slave labor, or wages no better, as well as other cost advantages and various subsidies of mind-boggling proportions.

Is re-training an answer?

Re-training whom for what and when? That is the real issue! If we are concerned about the people who have become unemployed (or "disemployed," as the snake oil salesmen put it) by downsizing, leveraged buyouts and worse in companies selling American jobs and the American market abroad—re-training assuredly is not an answer. Re-gaining those lost jobs is. That means re-capturing our lost manufacturing base. In the event that re-training were for the next generation, it could be helpful if it were for the right jobs. It is not. The proposed and available re-training is for the unemployed right now, to give them skills that many will not be able to master, and if they can master them, for jobs from which many would be excluded for various reasons not the least of these age, personal history (criminal or other unsavory record), and so forth.

Unbelievable, and equally nonsensical, is the fact that the training is for the "post-industrial era," a "high-tech society," and a "service economy"—the Reagan Administration's projected future and dangerous fantasy. This truth is inescapable even if such a future were viable, which it isn't given our experience and history—our own and that of others. The realistic present cannot, and should not, be replaced by a future possibility, however idealistically it may be viewed.

The existing problem, with far worse to come, will not be solved by job opportunities like flipping hamburgers in fast-food franchises on Main Street or any other street, the communications super-highway of the Internet, or even less by the dirty deals on Wall Street with their world-wide ramifications. The issue is jobs right now, not a generation or more in the future. And *real* jobs will demand a manufacturing base, not the flim-flam of financial manipulation as the guiding star of this nation. Manufacturing is critical not only for *real* jobs and a healthy economy, but literally for our very ability to defend this country. That manufacturing capacity is rapidly disappearing and with it our capability to defend ourselves. Buying our military requirements from potential adversaries is not exactly a wise choice. In truth, it could be the death-knell of this great country.

Far worse, such a strategy simply writes off the "disemployed" of right now—the age fifties, probably even the forties plus; the high school graduates; the illiterates; the dropouts; the unskilled, semi-skilled, even certain highly skilled of virtually any age; the inner city population; probably a lot of lower and middle managers; and on and on. Clearly, re-training isn't going to make even a minor dent in the short term.

The Reagan administration literally had no solutions to these absolutely basic and vital questions.

    (1) What industries will replace our lost industries?

(2) From where will the trillions of dollars for replacement industries come?

(3) What is to be done with our "disemployed" millions of people in the intervening ten to twenty years, if you have answers to the first two questions?

They had *no* answers to any of the questions!

The Clinton administration has been equally fatuous and irresponsible in this respect. It has spent billions on re-training for jobs that don't exist and often for people who wouldn't qualify even if the jobs did exist. In short, they are simply compounding the problem.*

At the same time, these administrations (along with their Republican and other cohorts) have been shipping out jobs that Americans, in dire need, can do—moving them to Mexico, the Far East, Southeast Asia, South America, and any place else imaginable, any place that has cheap labor, with a tip of their black hats to NAFTA, GATT, and our foreign competitors. In the midst of all this, too little constructive complaint has been heard from too much union leadership! Why? It's hard to understand, because it seems to be a direct contradiction of the union role in protecting American jobs.

Despite protestations to the contrary, the UAW-CIO has not been lily-white in this regard. Union support for re-training has to be political or worse. Lack of a grasp on reality would seem unlikely!

---

*Sad to say, since this book was written, government irresponsibility has continued. Under all of Clinton and Bush II the pattern has remained the same.

All of these people, sadly, have forgotten which flag to salute and where the first call on their loyalty lies when they contemplate the "global market" and the "new world order." Under a false face of patriotism and the phony pretext of economic efficiency, they are "selling" American jobs and selling out America.

Is re-training a solution? It might be if you don't need a job; if you can wait ten or twenty years to get one (or maybe if you are not yet born); if you have a job that is guaranteed for life; if you have a large Swiss bank account; if your need or desire is for a low-paying, temporary, part-time, or service job (with few or no benefits); and, most important, if you don't care about this country, its people, its one-time standard of living for all Americans, its future, and its dream (the American Dream)!

CHAPTER 3

"ECONOMICS" TODAY? NONSENSE!

World War I winners lost and losers won!

"Economics" in this country used to mean good jobs for everyone; the highest standard of living in the world for our people; and the American Dream as an inspiration to the people of this nation and also as an aspiration for people the world over. Such was our country's situation following World War II and probably until the 1970s. Then a horrendous change occurred, but the beginnings of this change actually date much further back, to the late stages of World War II itself when planning for the post-war era had begun. Although we won that war militarily, the story—tragically—did not end there. We lost (and continue to lose despite our times of seeming affluence) the economic war.

President Harry Truman, General Douglas MacArthur, Secretary of Defense and then State (former General) George Marshall and others of similar inclination believed that the victorious United States should put back together what it (and the Allies) had rent asunder. Despite the obviously hateful acts of our enemies (and unfortunately one major ally as well, namely the Soviet Union), our munificence was boundless for these former deadly foes.

However, it was not so for our war-time allies who held the world together for us until we decided that maybe there was a need for us to involve ourselves and help save the bacon—most particularly our own. After the war ended and when its costs had devastated these allies, our position was, "We'd really like to help you financially, but we can't. Why? Because you're an imperial power."

This was foolish and catastrophic naiveté, since these countries were the glue for the rest of the world. That glue dried out disastrously and the world broke apart. The need for a post-war buffer against the Soviet Union was clear, but the highly touted Marshall Plan was not the only option. Exercising that option was very costly in many ways, despite its being sanctified by many countries, including our own, and most of the world's luminaries. However, from a competitive standpoint, the economic costs of implementing the Marshall Plan were ultimately enormous, but even today are not generally understood, much less conceded.

What did America lose?
The peace and millions of jobs!

These undoubtedly well-meaning American leaders unbelievably forgot the primary point of warfare. You must win the long-term peace—not just the war. Otherwise, what you have won is not only a hollow victory but, worse still, a peace in name only.

Lots of notables claim we won the peace. In many ways we did—for a goodly while. After all, they say, look at our growth and financial gains. It was true for a long time, but time has finally caught up with us. Our markets have been invaded, our *real* jobs sacrificed, a large part of our actual wealth lost, and the very way of life in America jeopardized. These devastations have occurred both at the hands of former enemies (Japan and Germany primarily) *and* putative allies (e.g. China, Korea, Taiwan, India, etc.).

Other problems of a parallel nature have been caused in large part by the utter greed for money and power of many among our own so-called leaders in the various areas of our lives from government (administrations and congresses) to "global" corporations right here at home, to Wall Street's investment houses and brokerage firms, to banks and other financial enterprises ad infinitum.

What we have (and have had) really isn't peace at all but another form of warfare, and we don't mean the "cold war." Rather it is "economic warfare," which can ultimately be much worse than the cold war or even actual warfare in some ways.

However, over too many years the "leaders" of this country and their media mouthpieces have, at all costs, avoided calling it what it is. The reason? Their fears that their political, business and personal interests might be damaged if they did.

We should have understood something pretty simple and basic: "Treat your enemies' wounds, but remember they were (and are) the enemy. They killed and maimed millions. Don't restore them to a position of full-strength warriors—militarily or otherwise." We missed the point and did the exact opposite, making them economic warriors who in

time invaded our markets and undermined our
manufacturing economy. Later some actually took
our jobs (aided and abetted by our "leaders") to
their own countries while other countries also saw
the opportunity and took it.

Enemies' fault?
Not really. We helped them do it to us!

There were many economic rationalizations.
One was that we needed to rebuild these enemy nations in order to develop markets for our products.
Another was that they needed economic stability in
order for us to have "peace." There were further rationalizations of fairness and conscience. In addition, there was the pragmatic consideration of making enemies, such as Germany and Italy, into allies
(buffers) against the Soviet Union, once we had
agreed to Soviet dominion over what became their
new sphere of influence (Eastern Europe). Japan
was made into an ally as a way to protect U.S. interests in the Far East.

There was a degree of merit in a number of
these contentions. The sorry truth is that we went
overboard to the extreme. Moderation, or other
buffer options, would have done the job and averted
the problem.

In due course, the upshot of our post-war
largesse (and overt industrial espionage by our former enemies) was the underwriting by the United
States of virtually all new manufacturing facilities in
Japan and Germany that ultimately enabled them to
produce better products than we could. Furthermore, they could make their products cheaper because of these more efficient facilities and far lower

total labor costs. We continued to operate with mostly old plants and equipment plus higher payments to our workforce. However, we did not start to take a serious beating until twenty or twenty-five years later, because during the interim our sheer size, momentum, capital, and marketing know-how protected us. But our undoing was predictable, and predicted, as far back as when the Volkswagen "Beetle" got one half of 1 percent of the American automobile market in the early 1950s. By the end of that decade, after the firm of Doyle Dane Bernbach took over the advertising for the car, it had begun to appeal to large numbers of Americans. (Doyle Dane Bernbach started the use of the name "Beetle" in its advertising for the Volkswagen.)

In time came the flood! Why?

Then, and particularly by the 1970s, various areas of American business began to be hurt (automobiles, electronics, steel, and others). We let foreign products come into our market—remember, still far and away the world's biggest—virtually without limit and with practically no significant financial constraints. Despite Washington's protestations to the contrary, Presidents Nixon to Carter to Reagan to Bush I, and—still worse—to Clinton, "free-trade" actions disguised economic warfare. Subsequent policy failures have continued to devastate our country and its people!

One very early example of the new economic war occurred in Detroit during the late 1940s when I was working for Ford. What took place then was an indicator of the tactics that would eventually give rise to the economic problems we have been and are experiencing. Japanese visitors came through all the Ford plants at the River Rouge industrial complex (the world's largest at that time) in Dearborn, Michigan, on a non-stop basis and in endless numbers. Each of them had a camera and photographed everything in sight.

Having fought the Japanese for many years in World War II, several of us (in what was called The Ford Field Training Program) were less than admirers of their national character. At the same time, respect for their perseverance and shrewdness was very high. So, observing these photographic forays in the Detroit area, it seemed that we at Ford were being more than a little foolish to permit such overt industrial spying. We confronted the bosses with this issue. Their response essentially was "Don't worry about it. The Japanese just make plastic junk!" In those days that was true. However, we tried to explain that this would not always be the case. "They are smart, tough, and take the long view. These film safaris are designed to knock us off in their own time."

Those exhortations incredibly fell on deaf ears. Because the bosses had not been in the war, they didn't believe what was actually occurring. Nor did they pass our point of view up the line for whatever reasons. Even if they had, perhaps nothing would have been done anyway. Very likely there was a national three-monkeys policy for our former enemies—"See, hear, speak no evil." Regardless, the same thing was happening all over Detroit, and nobody apparently cared. Undoubtedly around the rest of the country, numerous other industries had the same experience. Otherwise, many of our industries in so many fields could not have been totally destroyed.

So began the unforeseen and undetected loss of good jobs in manufacturing for Americans; the erosion of the world's highest standard of living; and the disappearance of the American Dream—the dream that was a reality! Whose fault was this? We once thought it was all that of the Japanese and Germans along with their cohorts.

Then the realization dawned that they were simply operating in their own national self-interest—which they should have been. We were, and are, the ones who let them get away with it. "We have met the enemy, and they are us" (courtesy of Snoopy?). After all, the United States government didn't seem to care. In fact, it appeared to be supporting this frontal industrial piracy.

Who really loses? Working people in America! Who wins? The American "elite" and foreigners!

Starting with the Reagan administration (and continuing through subsequent administrations), "economics" in this country has meant good jobs for some; no jobs for others; part-time, temporary and low-paying jobs for too many. Our standard of living has deteriorated in a major way for most people and been elevated to "royal" status for some who have been the basic destroyers of our way of life. The last group includes those successive administrations in Washington as well as many Wall Streeters, bankers, downsizing CEOs who have displaced millions of American jobs by sending the work "offshore," members of congress (going back through many congresses) in great but not total measure, politicians at other government levels, academics, and on and on. The American Dream has become a fantasy for most and a nightmare for many. Truly a tragic farce!

All through the early 1990s, and often before, we have been told by Washington and the media how wonderful the economy is and how rosy the future appears. We have had the lowest unemployment percentage (not numbers) in years, stable interest rates, an ever ascending stock market! All true, but for whose benefit? And how long will this state of affairs last?

The benefit is for "investors." Most Americans are not active investors, despite the propaganda about people's "indirect investment" in pension funds, retirement plans, mutual funds, and so forth. But the "manna from heaven" with regard to the stock market and the economy cannot continue indefinitely.*

The countries that have pre-empted our manufacturing industries are taking even more of them and our service industries too. These countries want our market, but only as long as it is more lucrative than the markets we have created with the "offshore" jobs that replaced U.S. jobs assuming such a choice ever is required (God forbid!).

Numerous "economists," academics and other "experts" bear witness to "facts" when they are the opposite of the truth. (And too many obfuscate, if not worse, their views about these two critical areas—the economy and the stock market—or tem-

---

*Note that in fact it did not continue indefinitely. Within a few short years, the bubble burst, and it was not just the "investors" but rather the average American who really suffered.

porize in responding to questions about them. Some are blind; others are oblivious, often intentionally. This is truly voodoo economics—not George H. W. Bush assessing Reaganomics before joining that administration, but a devastating line of propaganda to mislead the American people for the benefit of a relatively few selfish, greedy, avaricious so-called Americans.

One of the non-Americans benefitting from our seeming naiveté—which is actually quite the opposite on the part of the people determining U.S. policy—is mentioned in this amusing but telling little story. An American businessman visiting Taiwan was invited to dinner at the home of some friends. Noticing Florida souvenir placemats on the table, he asked his hosts when they had visited Florida. "Oh, we've never been there," the woman replied. "My husband makes them."

Humorous story? Yes. However, the moral is anything but—particularly if you have tried to buy "American" in recent years, or if you have been downsized, "re-engineered," or whatever the current buzzword is these days for being thrown into the street with no job prospects, much less opportunities.

What happened to
the common sense of economics?
It was ignored, rejected, subverted!

There was "economics" common sense that was absolutely clear many years ago. It went totally unheeded but could have counteracted the effects of our failure to win the long-term peace after World War II. That tragic loss unfortunately was not visible to most people in the form of the economic decisions made at the time nor later during the ensuing economic war that has been labeled "free-market" economics. Free, that is for our foreign competitors and many seemingly "American" companies. As pointed out earlier, these "American" companies are selling, in some cases, foreign goods under American names or, in other instances, supposedly American products made of all or largely foreign components that have been assembled in the United States.

It is anything but free, however, when devastating slave-labor foreign competition faces some truly American companies in their own backyard. These American companies are making American products with American workers. Are even such American companies totally without fault? Sometimes not. In various instances, they are forced to use imported parts for various reasons—mostly price. But their degree of responsibility is little more than a drop in the ocean by comparison with the off-shoring of jobs by those who do so for pure and simple greed..

It is painfully true that there are far too many American companies of a vastly different stripe which are guilty as sin. These are generally companies that consider themselves "global" and are more concerned about their companies' interests (and their executives' personal gain) than about the needs of our country. They actually see themselves as more important than the good of the very nation, itself. So, you can imagine where U.S. employees, U.S. customers, U.S. suppliers, U.S. any and everything else (except Wall Street!) fit into the list of priorities for such companies. Not very high up, you can be certain! Yet, many such companies bear the best known corporate names in the history of American business. Hardly the stuff of principles by which a successful country remains a success. What a tragic and shameful commentary!

Here is the common sense, not nonsense, of economics for us, the people, and for our once great country. And great it will be again if you and enough of our fellow Americans refuse to let the self-serving money grubbers continue to take it away from us. (There are some action steps with which we can prevent these "legal" crimes. You can find them toward the end of this book.)

How can this state of affairs exist? Largely because most of these companies have been taken over in one way or another by less than desirable investment "firms" or groups (often with the involvement of large foreign interests), and with the complicity of major law firms. These groups usually know nothing (and could not care less) about the company except for its assets and profitability, otherwise known by the financial cliché as the "bottom line." However, they know how to get their people on boards of directors, and they do it. These directors pick the top management. Another thing they know is the value for each of the company's various pieces, which they will sell off to recover their "investment."

Their only real question is: "What did you do for me yesterday—in forcing greater profits or stock value out of the business (and into my pocket, that is)?" Why are there no restrictions on these people except for a few token constraints?

We should ask our government (Administration and Congress)! Unhappily, the answer would be so devised, with endless words, that the answer is sure to come out as no answer. The reason? The investment "industry" and its foreign participants have the necessary influence in the government to get the "laws" they want, because you and I, and the rest of our fellow citizens, allow it to happen. In short, the plunderers have access to the people who write as well as pass such legislation, and the resources, used in one way or another, to influence the decisions in their favor. None of this is a secret. It's documented up one side and down the other in endless books and articles. Consider only "campaign reform" as an example of words used with the intention of conveying the exact opposite impression of the reality.

Anyway, such is the harsh truth that has to be pretty clear to anyone who is willing to give even a little thought to the situation. It is very strange that no one has put the true onus (monkey!) where it belongs. I wonder why? Money, power, control? Sadly, too often all three of them! Our families' very lives, not to mention livelihoods, have been in their hands. "If you control the purse, you control those it feeds!" So, most of us have gone along with what we have been told on the basis that our "leaders" (government, finance, business, academia, media, unions, etc.) must know what they are doing. Unfortunately, they do, without doubt, but what is being done isn't in our interests or this nation's! Rather, it's for their own greedy, self-serving purposes. Exceptions? Of course, but far too few.

CHAPTER 4

AMERICA WORKS WHEN AMERICANS WORK!
IT DOESN'T WHEN THEY DON'T!
AND IT ISN'T WORKING!

In a basic sense, here is the real problem underlying all of our economic woes. As we have lost important industries, in whole or in part, to other countries and those industries were not replaced (as they have not been in real terms) we also lose:

(1) companies,
(2) the income from those companies,
(3) the jobs they provided,
(4) the personal income of the people who held the jobs,
(5) the former companies' buying power,
(6) the buying power of former companies' suppliers, plus their jobs and income,
(7) those companies' and job holders' taxes (additional buying power for our governmental units with which they create jobs and more spending power outside of government by buying goods and services from private business) and paying

for the labor and material that go into building such things as bridges, roads, airports, etc.).

How can consumers without jobs buy anything? They can't!

Two-thirds of our national income (so-called GDP, Gross Domestic Product) is supposed to come from consumer buying. How can consumers continue buying to the same extent with ever-shrinking consumer income? The answer is obvious and devastating; they can't. The present administration and its two predecessors have religiously rejected these harsh but inevitable realities. Their claim is that "We are now a service economy." For how long before these jobs are out-sourced? And we are rapidly on the way to becoming a nation with ever less well-paying jobs. So, we have jobless people, homeless people, hungry people, frightened people. And a few richer-than-Croesus people!

Our lost industries are legion, as is painfully evident: possibly as much as half, if not more, of the automobile industry in a truthful analysis (for decades the dynamo of the economy), makers of TV sets, radios, electronics, steel, tires and other rubber products, micro-chips (lost and recouped), appliances, computers, textiles, apparel, shoes, and on and on—not to mention the profit from foreign capital investments in our own country (both the interest on debt, national as well as other, and commercial enterprises). As profits from foreign products, services, and investments plus interest on debt leave our country, our jobs and our income are still further reduced. The reason is that this money is simply not available to create and build enterprises in the U.S. which could in turn provide jobs.

When we don't buy American (real American), what happens? We dig our own graves (financially) and volunteer to be slaves (economically and, maybe in due course, literally)!

When we don't buy or try to buy (or try to buy and can't find) a radio or TV set or clothes or shoes or anything else made in the United States, purchases of foreign products have these results:

(1) We are not buying from ourselves (something made in the U.S.).

(2) We are destroying American jobs—our jobs.

(3) We are reducing the income of Americans—our income.

(4) We are lowering the standard of living of Americans—our standard of living.

(5) We are destroying the United States and its people—our country and our lives.

In time, and sooner rather than later, failure to "build American" and "buy American" will result in failure to rebuild and/or replace U.S. industry. No jobs for you and me; no income for us. Both of these facts mean no way to buy anything for our families and ourselves from anywhere, be it made here or elsewhere!

In other words, using a car as an example, we are better off buying a real American car (even assuming it is not quite as good as an import, which certainly need not be the case and in certain instances probably isn't) than a foreign-made one. If we don't, we'll eventually have no jobs, no income, and no buying power to buy any car, made here or in another country, much less anything else. Isn't something, even if possibly "not quite as good" now, better than no car of any kind at that early future point? Remember—if we lose the American automobile industry (assuming truly American: made in America by Americans from American components) *and others*, we lose not only those companies, but also the companies that supply parts as well as materials and services to them—all companies that provide many of us with our livelihoods either directly or indirectly. This compounding effect would destroy our nation as we have known it. This essential manufacturing base and critical defense capability will perish all too soon. It is rapidly happening each and every day. Our very life-blood is being drained without even the slightest notice, far be it a warning.

Why are we not told this simple truth?
Truth is dangerous!

Why then do our country's "leaders," economists, media, and all those others who should do so not tell us, the people, these crystal clear realities? Is it because there are no solutions? Absolutely not! There are. They simply don't want us to know, or they don't want us to know that they don't know. The truth is that these erstwhile leaders have to be misguided, befuddled, stupid, inordinately pressured by their own self-interest or consumed with lining their own pockets by selling out our country and us. Take your choice!

Are there solutions? Of course!

Various short-term solutions to the economic woes of our "disemployed" and underemployed people (e.g., tax cuts and rebates, selective interest rate reductions, investment tax credits, quotas, tariffs, public investment programs, and so on) have been proposed. Some combination is vital for the immediate future of our citizens who are truly in desperate straits right now. However, most of these measures are merely holding actions. Furthermore, they often increase the deficit and national debt, since the funding is from public monies. Certainly a quick, albeit temporary, solution is badly needed. However, a *basic solution* must be undertaken in short order if we are not to jump off the precipice of economic suicide but instead climb back to the solid ground of a soundly growing and prosperous country. This is a structural problem, *not* a cyclical one.

**What are longer-run remedies
to recover real jobs?
Incentives and penalties!**

One approach to a fundamental remedy would provide incentives for both U.S. manufacturers and consumers over a reasonable period of time—until American manufacturers' products meet the purchase requirements of customers at all distribution levels from industrial to retail. Another approach would impose severe penalties for job reductions from off-shoring. Or—better still!—both. In such ways, *real* jobs can be restored to America by rebuilding lost industries (sufficient time needed) in this country, with full-time jobs being returned from overseas and reborn here. Incentives for manufacturers could be investment tax credits or other forms of subsidy for domestic production.

The incentive approach for consumers/retail and wholesale purchasers (including manufacturers' purchases) could be a fixed percentage off the list price of a truly U.S. product (to be defined in detail) from a really U.S. company (to be specified very clearly and carefully) in the form of a tax credit or an immediate federal government rebate to that buyer (be it a manufacturer, wholesaler, retailer, or consumer) or something of a similar nature. In other words, one would get a "break" on an American product that is actually "made in the USA"! (Note that a financial projection model for the automobile industry at this time actually exists—but utilizes only positive incentives. Even without other incentives, it produces a handsome profit all round, including one for the U.S. Government.)

The incentives program would not and should not impede or affect the usual negotiations between seller and buyer with regard to price determination. It would simply be an additional price reduction. The credit or rebate has to be a totally independent consideration. Accordingly, the U.S. would not be imposing quotas or similar "onerous" restrictions on imports but simply helping our own economy with our own money and our own ingenuity. Heresy to many? Without doubt! Better heresy, though, than disaster! The heresy group, by the way, is the plundering elitists and their beneficiaries, not the true Americans who want to see our nation and its people once more flourish with the American Nightmare of the present replaced by the lost American Dream. You might ask those who cry protectionism if they believe that being able to defend our nation, and our very lives, is protectionist. In the event they do, try the word "survival" on them. Should they not get that, then don't waste your time with such people. Suicide is a bad option!

Is this incentives idea feasible?
Yes—with hard work!

The amount of the credit or rebate would have to be determined by a financially supportable formula—industry by industry. This could be done on the basis of projected increases in jobs; additional personal, business, and other taxes; unemployment savings; and other considerations as well. If foreign manufacturers can subsidize exports to our market as they do, we can and certainly had better equalize our domestic product costs now and thereby counter the unfair price differences—GATT and NAFTA notwithstanding! The fact is that we have already waited far too long.

Given such an impetus, the problems of real unemployment and underemployment, reduced standard of living and all the others mentioned could be turned around (not overnight but on a forced draft basis). Most important, we also would be able to put our country permanently back on its feet.

Furthermore, the additional advantage of this strategy is that it pays for itself. It not only doesn't increase the deficit (not to mention the national debt), it actually reduces that problem in very large part and eventually could eliminate it. The strategy does so not by smoke and mirrors, manipulation of the wrong taxes and interest rates (which obviously

doesn't work), or dirty deals on Wall Street and selling T-shirts (made in China) on Main Street, but by
restoring our capacity to make things for our own
enormous market and the international one too.
Making things here makes *real* jobs here.

Are there strict requirements
for manufacturers?
Very strict requirements!

Manufacturers must know that these measures
are for truly domestic products only, not products
and parts made elsewhere that bear a U.S. company's name or products made elsewhere that are
simply assembled here. Manufacturers also must
know that there is a specific cut-off date for the incentives period—that is, to meet consumer purchase requirements without the price break.

There should be scheduled incentive decreases
to promote effectiveness and efficiency as the program proceeds. At the cut-off time, a manufacturer
has to be able to compete on its own without this
advantage. However, if it can't, it will not be permitted to resort to foreign outsourcing of labor,
parts, and so forth. Labor, wholesale customers, retail consumers, investors, and all other concerned
parties need to know these things as well, in order
to monitor the situation and thereby protect their
own interests. In other words, producers must do
the job right and be competitive at the cut-off point
or face the consequences of a cut-off in business.

To bring such a program into being, the federal
government (the Administration and Congress) has
to move expeditiously and effectively in conjunction with management and labor to implement de-

tailed plans industry by industry and to put these plans to work on an expedited basis. This strategy is not "protectionism." It is really the opposite—to change our current self-destruct course so that this country heads back to a sound and healthy condition with *real* jobs for the American people and not temporary, part-time, low-paying jobs or, worse still, no jobs.

Such *real* industrial jobs are particularly important for all the groups of people who have been, or will be, annihilated by the current "service" economy course this country's policymakers—our so-called leaders—are following. The individuals in these groups needing good jobs now number untold millions.

Sooner or later, this misbegotten "service" economy of ours (in the so-called post-industrial era the government and many economists proclaim as nirvana) is going to run out of anything to service in this country. The time is soon approaching when we will be totally replaced by other countries in making things. Then our service industries will have only these foreign countries to service. So, at that point we will be completely dependent upon them and, therefore, virtually enslaved. The final step will be when they decide to provide those services for themselves. At such time, we will be finished completely—if we permit the continuation of such folly which clearly we must stop, in one way or another.

Everything here deals with our vitally important need for jobs. Unfortunately, it doesn't even touch on our critical defense requirements. Tackling that all-important subject must wait for another time.

For the moment, suffice it to say that with the self-destruction of this country's manufacturing base, soon we shall be able to produce even less of what is critically necessary for the defense of our very own nation. Obviously the dangers of making such vital items in foreign countries (some potential enemies) and then transporting them from those countries here are only too clear. In short, make it here or die—economically or, worse still, literally! That's what we must realize.

CHAPTER 5

INCENTIVE OR PENALTY FOR AMERICAN BUSINESS?
BOTH!

**Does this incentive idea affect our "free market?"
No, because a "free market" doesn't really exist
in the United States!**

It is true that this course does not provide a
"free market"; rather, it creates an equitable market, a fair market. Our so-called free market isn't
really free, despite the claims, except for the predators of both U.S. and foreign origin. It has all
kinds of biases and distortions, such as foreign
subsidies for products brought into this country;
foreign and American-owned plants in the United
States that use parts made in other countries under
subsidies; American and foreign companies that
use Mexico and Japan, along with many additional
Asian countries, for cutting labor costs of products
sold in the United States (thanks even more so to
NAFTA in the case of Mexico) and on and on.

We also should not forget that the profits of
foreign-owned companies (and those with plants in
the U.S.) go back to those countries. Such profits

do not benefit America; for example, the profit from the sale of a Toyota in the United States goes back to Japan; the profit from the sale of a Mercedes goes back to Germany.

Shouldn't there also be a penalty program for job losses in the U.S.?
Without doubt!

There should be another program that penalizes companies heavily for every American job lost to a foreign country. (This program ought to be in addition to the incentive program outlined in the previous chapter.) However, the problem of getting such legislation through Congress would be even greater than with the first program, and that problem is enormous in its own right. Yet, it should somehow be shoved down Congress's throat, regardless, to stop the unconscionable destruction of American workers and their families! If enough of us acted together, such leverage might force the necessary legislation.

Unquestionably, a penalty program is in order in conjunction with the incentive program. It's about time that this country looked after its own people first, as it once did. Only then can we worry about others (and we should, but not until the time is right). Unhappily we have forgotten the old adage, "Charity begins at home." Nevertheless, a realistic assessment of our Congress almost certainly rules a penalty program out at this juncture—unless overwhelming herculean pressure from the people (more than offsetting current monetary contributions from vested interests) can be brought to bear. Highly unlikely!

Who comes first? Americans or others? Wake up, America!

The real issue is, first of all, to ensure the well-being of Americans and to bring back the American standard of living before it is lost once and for all. So, this nation's truly critical mission is not to provide jobs for the rest of the world. Rather it is, first and foremost, to have *good* jobs for Americans. After that, we can look after the interests of people in other countries.

However, those interests will not be served by countenancing the use of slave labor abroad, nor by rewarding the foreign employment of child labor at $1 a day. Worse still is to sanction the use of child labor at the expense of jobs (paying a few cents more) for such children's parents. The guise too often used is that it's better for a family to have some income (even if it comes from child labor) than no income. These practices are not only an abomination, but they are also an abject disgrace to humanity! In short, they are a complete denial of our own absolutely basic tenets of life and values.

It is often argued that people are better off having jobs at slave-labor rates than no jobs at all. True. Unfortunately, though, these jobs are at the cost of American jobs at fair labor rates! That cost is unjustified when America's first responsibility is to Americans. (Certainly slave labor anywhere is unconscionable, but our conscience must first tackle the plight of America.) Furthermore, the profit from such exploitation only too frequently goes to American corporate profiteers ("global corporations") who prey upon American consumers by touting lower prices but failing to mention the costs. Those costs are not only lost American jobs but also impoverished families. They no less include the horrors of foreign slave labor in too many cases—child abuse, horrific dangers, health destruction, prison conditions, and so forth.

What are U.S. "leaders" doing to Americans and others?

Our "leaders" are riding to glory (using abhorrent practices for one purpose—money grubbing) on the backs of these poor benighted souls in economically backward or dictator-dominated nations. Furthermore, these decision-makers don't give a second thought to (or give a good damn about) the millions of Americans who, thanks to the decisions made by the powers that be, have been made redundant, downsized, or re-engineered. In whatever buzzword of the current self-protection jargon, our leaders have denied *real* jobs for *real* Americans and killed the American Dream! In short, they have deprived many millions of Americans of any job—and therefore of even a remotely decent way of life. A travesty of leadership and a tragedy for our nation and its people!

So, a penalty program could help in reversing this descent into disaster for our country. Some of the program's provisions should include a variety of disincentives for the exponents of the godforsaken policies and practices that are selling the people of this once great industrial dynamo right down the proverbial river.

For what should U.S. companies face penalties? Job losses!
What kind of penalties? Severe and harsh!

U.S. companies should pay stiff financial penalties (to be determined by competent, impartial decision makers) on a damage inflicted scale for:

- every job added outside of the United States to produce products for the U.S. market
- every existing job outside of the United States dedicated to producing products for the U.S. market
- every non-citizen (unless no qualified U.S. citizen is available) working in the United States for a U.S. company
- every job lost in the United States unless the company can prove that the job will not be replaced outside of the United States in a subsidiary, in a foreign company from which it buys, or in some form of joint venture in which it has an interest
- every product that could be made in the United States but is brought into the United States by a company in which any U.S. company has a substantial interest or investment (to be stated in very specific terms)
- every product, that could be (and earlier was) made here, brought into the U.S., and sold by a U.S. company
- and any other such situations of similar nature that are omitted here

Many business "leaders," in general, and not just importers and retailers, are sure to be heard screaming like wounded elephants, "Such a plan destroys import and retail jobs." "It will kill export markets and jobs." "Prices are going to be higher." All true to some degree. However, the jobs added—*real* jobs, not low-paying service jobs (many of which are part-time, or temporary in stores, restaurants, etc., a point that cannot be restated too often)—inevitably are going to be much greater in number (and pay!). There simply is no valid argument to the contrary unless one uses "lies, damned lies and statistics" (which are often accurate in this order!).

Prices probably would be somewhat higher in the short term—but not for long. For example, TV sets (originally made in this country) cost a lot when they were first introduced. Then domestic competition grew, volume increased, and prices dropped dramatically. The situation under the proposed conditions would be similar. The ramp-up time for certain industries would be substantially longer, however, in order to restore our basic manufacturing capability. Still, it's better to have higher prices and jobs that provide money to pay them than lower prices, no jobs, and no money to pay any price, regardless of how low such prices are. These points apply to the real people of this country, not to the so-called "leaders" and that favored small percentage (getting, not "making" unconscionable amounts of money) who are dragging us ultimately into the abyss of national economic disaster and personal financial catastrophe.

What kinds of penalties would there be for a company that reduces American jobs (without a legitimate reason—reduction of direct labor cost, absent valid basis, not being one)? Tough penalties!

Lost job penalties could be determined through various formulas dependent upon the nature of the situation. The basis might be something like this:

- For a lost job, take total compensation (yearly salary + benefits).
- Multiply that total by some factor(s) contingent upon the circumstances of the job being lost— moved to another country; sold in effect to a foreign producer; or whatever the reason.
- Add the resulting amount to the company's taxable income for X years, say five (possibly somewhere between three to ten); or add it to the company's actual tax for X years (in either event, enough to be a severe disincentive).

What kinds of incentives would there be for a company that adds jobs? Big incentives!

Quite simply, the penalties for companies that destroy jobs could be reversed for companies that increase jobs. And again, the formulas should follow essentially the same ground rules, but flip-flopped so that on this side of the coin major incentives would be available. In addition, a distinction should be made between manufacturing and service jobs so that manufacturing jobs have a substantial, but fair, premium.

Are these ideas to regain real jobs for Americans going to meet with resistance? Yes. Enormous resistance!

The hue and cry in the United States and around the world from the "destroyers" who are consumed by greed at our expense will be deafening. Doesn't matter! The people of this country deserve to know the truth that they seldom, if ever, get. Given the facts, Americans will make the right judgments. With wrong, and often deliberately misleading, information no reasonable person is able to reach the right conclusion.

Critics will say that the proposed programs are anti–world free trade. The truth, of course, is that they are, to an extent, and they should be. It's about time that we learned "free trade" isn't free except as practiced in the United States for foreign (and U.S. offshore) predator competition. We finally must also realize that *real* jobs for Americans are critical to our economic survival.

Despite the contention that the U.S. job market is tight, this tightness exists only in certain skilled categories such as computer programming. It has nothing to do with other categories or the millions of people in the "disemployed," underemployed or unemployed categories, much less with the "overemployed and underpaid" who work several jobs for family survival and at rates far lower than they once earned. Thus, manufacturing must be restored in the United States to provide millions of *real* jobs for unskilled, semi-skilled, skilled, supervisory, and managerial workers. Failing this, the country will fail! No amount of sleazy, greedy, and corrupt financial manipulation will change that.

Wall Street and its cohorts will lead us only to disaster—not the pot of gold or the promised land!

Frighteningly, our "leaders" don't understand this basic reality or choose not to. Without a rebirth of manufacturing in this country, even these people's own selfish interests will not be served unless such interests are very, very short term indeed. Possibly having all their ill-gotten loot on a Swiss mountain top and having fled the destruction they wrought in the United States is how they want to live (assuming such a mountain top has not been leveled by a nuke and there is a thing called loot still in the safe-deposit vaults of the Zurich gnomes' unnumbered accounts).

Critics will also say, as mentioned before, that these ideas would hurt our export business. They will for a time and to some degree. However, our total manufacturers' *export* business is $701.2 billion and our total manufactured *imports* are $807.4 billion. The trade deficit ($106.2 billion) is obviously very large.*

Which would you rather have? Not too difficult a choice, is it!

---

*The source for these figures is the U.S. Department of Commerce, the Economics and Statistics Administration, the Bureau of the Census, and the Bureau of Economic Analysis, "U.S. International Trade in Goods and Services—Annual Revision for 1994." The very large 1994 trade deficit would continue rise over the years, reaching a whopping $760 billion in 2006—*a tragically widening gap of catastrophic proportions!*

CHAPTER 6

AMERICAN PRODUCTS MEAN
REAL AMERICAN JOBS!

Why American products?
Because they provide *real* jobs!

Now it's late, but let's hope—and, I believe—not too late to regain the American market (and American jobs) for America. As said repeatedly, it is *still* the world's single largest market by far. If truly American-made products, not foreign ones, fill our stores and are bought by Americans, the American people will have *real* jobs—manufacturing jobs. If foreign products, or products that are claimed to be American but aren't, continue to be what is sold in this country, the jobs we have, if any, will be low-paying service jobs. And even they will disappear as other countries take those jobs too. We can't wait any longer, or there will be nothing for which to wait. The task will not be easy or without negative effects, but it can and has to be accomplished. We must rise to the occasion and get behind the right strategy to save America for Americans and for the American Dream.

**Where have these jobs gone? Who's to blame?
America's "leaders" are!
But we let them get away with it!**

Let's not blame the Japanese (or other nations) for doing what is in their interest—taking over our manufacturing base for much of what is sold in the United States. After all, we gave them the resources and mandate to do so after World War II (and have ever since). In short, we rebuilt their economies, as pointed out earlier. We also should not be deluded into believing either that the Japanese market is going to be opened to us substantially or that, even if it were, our problems would be miraculously solved in one fell swoop, as we are often led to believe. Now we simply need to do, and must do, what is in our own best interest at home!

We, and only we, can fix this critical problem. Let's do so before it's too late (and too late will come about too soon). We created the problem—we being our government, our financial community, our corporations, our unions et al.

The first step is for us to tell the Administration, our Senators and our Congresswomen and men that their job is to return the American market to American jobs! We must keep stating what should be their primary concern but obviously isn't. "America works for the vast majority of Americans when Americans work! It doesn't when they don't! And it isn't working!" (Nor will our government, our unions, our corporations—despite their grandiose, "global" market views and "to hell with American jobs"!) This first step unfortunately is almost certain to fail, but we should try it just to have that effort on record in order for the blame to fall where it so rightly belongs (and has for such a very, very long time).

Why is the problem not admitted and solved? Politics and greed!

The politics involved are the kind that, in far too many cases but not all, demand supporting the causes of supporters, not the interests and needs of America. The greed implied covers an almost limitless number of self-serving causes. As such, the problem is not exactly easy to admit. In fact, it is obscured at virtually any cost!

Unquestionably there are ideas other than those in this book that could bail out this American travesty of "economic success" and serve the *true* interests of the American people. Quite possibly, there are better ideas. The sorry truth, nonetheless, is that no ideas have been offered except for interest rate and tax reductions or "make-work" government efforts and re-training for jobs that don't exist. As often repeated, there have been no *real* job creation proposals for millions of real Americans with real problems—those more than fifty years old; high-school drop outs; those with high school degrees only; teenagers; unskilled, semi-skilled, and skilled workers; "downsized" managers; and on and on!

To reiterate: there are government claims of millions of jobs being created. This is probably true up to a point. But the claims don't say that these jobs are too often low-paying, part-time, temporary, and without benefits! Nor is there ever mention of the fact that such jobs are usually not even sufficient to cover normal population growth requirements. They also don't mention the jobs lost and what they paid. We hear a lot about re-training —for jobs that don't exist. No "data" appear to be available in relation to how many jobs are needed for a family to scrape by. If such data exists, that information is well hidden. Any such information would constitute a form of admission.

Such is the miserable state of the economy in our country. There is statistical gobbledygook for the delusion of the vast majority of Americans and the benefit of the relatively few high-flyers. Lots of theory, computer models and academic holier-than-thou pronouncements—but no practical, workable solutions!

We are told that this economy is in great shape. But the Commerce Department frequently says it has to redo the basis for its figures. Not too convincing a recommendation for their contention of economic health! They should talk to us, the real people, about the real situation rather than engaging in double-talk with Wall Street and its cohorts.

It is long past the time for us to turn the tables unless we are willing to accept a progressively disintegrating standard of living for most of us and the end of the American Dream for all of us. I'm not, and I'm sure you aren't. We don't want our children and grandchildren working for slave wages or having no jobs at all. So, we must force our government (and our corporations) to work first for America— not for their self-serving greed to get unconscionable amounts of money and power—and then for the world, in that order, not in the reverse as they now are wont to do in all too many cases.

**Will these ideas be warmly embraced?
No—not by the "plunderers!"
But yes—by Americans who care! Who are
scared! Who see their country of opportunity
becoming one of despair!**

It is important to say once more that importers,
retailers, and others will complain bitterly about the
strategies recommended here meaning higher prices
for Americans. It is also important, however, to understand that this need not be the case. Still, remember that even if it is the case for a relatively short
time, it is better that we have higher prices with jobs
and money to buy than *no jobs* and *no money* to buy,
no matter how low the price, which is where we are
heading. We must be prepared for "global" corpora-
tions/manufacturers (many—but not all) to cry that
these strategies would hurt them in world markets.
They won't in most cases, except for those who demand inordinate profits.

Nevertheless, we must impress upon them that
the American market comes first and that if such cor-
porations/manufacturers can't accept the conditions,
they will be required to forego the U.S. market and
operate elsewhere. They simply will not be able to
sell their products here. It is highly unlikely that
many would want to give up our much vaunted
world's single largest market. Any corporations/man-
ufacturers that choose to do so would take inordinate
risks and find themselves far from irreplaceable.

In the final analysis, there is but one basic question to be asked about the American economy. Is
this country's economy, our economy, supposed to
benefit the great majority or a very small minority
of Americans (the "elite") and the so-called "global

economy"? My answer, and I believe yours and that of most Americans, is simple and clear. It is that this economy is to benefit Americans, in general, not the limited few who sacrifice America, Americans, and the American Dream for their own personal greed. It is not for the benefit of "global" corporations that consider themselves more important than the nation itself. Nor is it for the benefit of a select few as the self-chosen anointed! However, there are too many Wall Street manipulators (maybe economic "terrorists" is a better term), their puppets, and others who are being allowed by our government to get away with economic murder in the present situation.* In many cases, these manipulators are actually encouraged and supported by the government. And they do so at *our* great expense.

The saga of Wall Street is a sad one. It once was a community dedicated to sound investment in America. In the past twenty to thirty or so years, what was a respected and vital function has become a pernicious gamblers' paradise for those with "inside" information that leads to "globalized greed" and to the destruction of the nation it once served so well. Are there exceptions? Of course. Just not enough!

Who are the puppets?
Several categories of the "plunderers!"
Among these puppet order-takers are:
- corporate management "downsizers," "lean and mean" so-called leadership (easiest way to show quick profit improvement)

---

*And the result has been the financial strangulation and economic chaos of the country and the world today.

- manufacturer and other business management "yes men" and "yes women" (any damage is OK if it helps him or her)
- importers who believe that "all's fair in love and war" with them adding "and business" to the quote (*and* like-minded business) types
- retailers who are "beat American prices" disciples
- government and congressional collaborators
- foreign interests; and probably too many others

Their most evil calling, as stated before, is to capitalize on foreign "slave" labor at the expense of American jobs and America's future. The common denominator among them all is that they are "me-firsters." Not exactly the highest echelon of humanity!

Some of these people also employ still more soul-searing, cost-cutting devices (relating to the environment, health, safety and other human welfare needs) in any foreign country willing to accept them. Some of these devices are legal; some are not. These "advantages" are obtained at the cost of destroying the American economy, our lives, and, unless something is done, the lives of more generations to come than we can imagine, not to mention the dangers to foreign labor.

"It's the economy, stupid!"
But which economy?

The Clinton campaign had the problem right. However, the Clinton Administration "forgot" which economy was involved. The American people thought he meant the U.S. economy, since he was running for president of this country, not China or Japan. "It's the economy, stupid" was the right idea, but for the wrong economy. It was not the world economy (or, as the "in" people like to call it, the "global economy"). That's where opportunists see quick payoffs (and "faster bucks").

The Clinton Administration lost track of where its loyalty was supposed to lie. It was helping other nations and U.S. "global" corporations take over many American markets while failing to support manufacturing in our own country.

Incidentally, for any of the doubters reading these words, it is suggested that they try to find American products (except food) in any store and see how many there are! Another interesting, but self-defeating experience is to try to find out how much of an "American" car is *actually* American.

What's America's economic reality? American jobs or disaster!

The reality for America and Americans is that it's *our* economy which must be the focus of a sound strategy. We cannot accept a sell-out by "American" companies or a buy-out by foreign interests. Truly American companies have to *make things, in America*, from largely American parts and materials, with American workers, things that can then be bought by American consumers (and international consumers as well). In this way, the profits can go toward further American advantages—capital investment, lower taxes, reduced deficit, pay-down of national debt, and so forth.

The jobs necessary are American jobs—the kinds of jobs that make it possible for Americans to buy goods and pay taxes. The people who have the jobs must be American workers making fair and reasonable incomes sufficient to buy American products and restore the American standard of living and the American Dream. If we stop the financial terrorists and their cohorts, the American economy can and will have that focus again—instead of continuing to be dismantled for the greater good of the "global economy" and its profiteers. Bear in mind that China, Japan, the "Asian Tigers" and all the rest are not too terribly worried about us as long as their exports to the United States continue at record levels.

We must again become self-sufficient, producing for our own livelihoods and defense needs as well as our nation's other requirements, including the nation's profit (surplus, not deficit). We should also be a country making way for imports in a fair and rational sense. A sound balance of international trade is essential. But a devastating onslaught of imports is self-defeating and ultimately disastrous!

What has happened to America's companies? They have been taken over by the financial "terrorists!"

GDP (Gross Domestic Product) really means the sum of the enterprise in a country. In our country, business is the essence of that enterprise. For the most part companies are the basic substance of business. Companies once operated for (generally in this order) the benefit of employees, customers, stockholders, suppliers, and the overall good of the society (all of us, that is).

Now too many American companies, by far, exist solely for the exorbitant profits paid to "stockholders" and management who are under the control of a small group of major "investors" ("financial terrorists") who also control the company management (such management's jobs and pay being dependent upon these "investors'" decisions at Board of Directors meetings). The ultimate criterion for these "investors" is the so-called bottom line (profit) that determines the stock's price or, in other words, "What did you do for me today, Mr. Chief Executive?" Not a very sound basis for a company's long-term welfare!

It is particularly unconscionable when the quickest, easiest way to a fast profit is to dump employees without replacing them (and working those who remain into the ground). Equally reprehensible is replacing qualified, long-term employees with cheap (and often incompetent) workers! This route to brainless, short-term profitability is almost always available and has become today's pattern (and panacea) for American management. It should be said that in some limited number of cases there is a legitimate reason to reduce the number of employees on a reasonable, fair, and gradual basis—but certainly not in the virtually overnight, wholesale slaughter that too often is practiced. Worse still, in these situations, is sending those jobs to foreign countries at "slave" wages, literally or figuratively. Also unacceptable is importing cheap foreign workers; it is especially pernicious when they replace Americans (who have often trained them)! Either way, these practices are not good for America.

How do these people live with themselves? They worship mammon and lie a lot!

However, for such "managers," America and American jobs are of no concern. What is of concern to these people, first and foremost, is the unconscionable size of their paychecks and the assurance of keeping them coming as long as possible. They sell out to greed! Such "management" will tell you that this dumping of workers ("downsizing," "re-engineering" or whatever candy-coated term they use to refer to it) is necessary to save the people who remain. "They wouldn't have jobs if we didn't make these cuts." Believable? Hardly—just talk to the people who are left and are being worked to death! At any rate, managers apparently salve their consciences with rationalizations of this kind and worse.

Why wasn't this need for fewer people (sometimes a legitimate need) seen along the way and planned for accordingly and gradually? It's very odd, too, that the people making these decisions and doing such rationalizing often are the people who didn't do the adjusting or whatever was really needed in a timely, considered fashion. In short, the very same people that were derelict and who made these heinous errors are the "managers" who keep their "executive positions." Worse, such "managers" are the people who hypocritically and callously throw other people out of their jobs with nothing but fatuous and pompous speeches or equally misleading press releases as their excuses. They lie a lot!

Who is to blame?
The financial "terrorists," the "management,"
all such "plunderers"?
To be sure, but so are we!

Shame on them! Worse, shame on us for letting them get away with it. We must stop them, end their criminally "legal" actions and fix a dire situation before it is too late, or there won't be anything left to fix. In this case soon is late but let's hope not too late. Sooner, we all know, beats later—certainly in this situation. America will have reverted back to the fate of ancient Rome (one major difference being that we have had not one Nero but many) if we don't put out the fire. We have the equipment to do so, but it must be turned on the fire—by us—or the United States will burn like Rome (only more fiercely and with limitless consequences).

Our only excuses, it seems, are two! Either we trusted the wrong people, or the right people to trust were not in the running.

In short, economics begins at home. As some of you may remember, we once had a saying that charity did too. True economics is people, jobs, our standard of living, the American Dream—not lies, damned lies and statistical gimmickry to prove that black is white. For unfortunate and less than commendable reasons, be they from too little grasp of the reality if one is charitable, or too much grasping of their self-serving ambitions if not, our "leadership" has chosen to sacrifice the economic good of the country. They have turned a blind eye to America's needs and sold out vital American values as well as the nation itself along with a very, very large percentage of its people. The sell-out has been both to foreign influences and to American "plunderers." A "legal" crime? Probably not, but an even worse crime nonetheless.

CHAPTER 7

THE SAD AND SORRY TRUTH
OF AMERICAN INDUSTRY AND ITS JOBS!

"Unemployed? Hungry? Eat your foreign car!" This was seen on a bumper sticker not too long ago. Unfortunately it tells a vital part of the story, since there will be no money to buy food or anything else in this country if we don't start making things again—many more of our own cars, their components, their parts, their assembly, and all the other products that used to be truly American.

The only exceptions to the beggared American populace will be the "plunderers," in the event we allow them to continue to prey upon the nation for their personal advantage. Should we be so foolish, where and how could they use their ill-gotten gains? No U.S. left! World haven? No! Without a healthy America and its enormous market for much of the world's production, most of the world will be sick. Inter-country trade and annual payment totals make this point rather clearly when the indirect influences can be discerned. These short-sighted, greedy reprobates will confront a desperate world with no hope of sanctuary! If we are that lunatic, we deserve what we get! And what we get will be nothing short of slavery and the wages it pays (considerably less than the wages of sin, it must be pointed out, if we are to keep something of a sense of humor in this tragic farce).

What are the real facts?
Bad and getting worse!

Without getting into the lies, damned lies, and statistics used by the government, Wall Street, politicians, the media, corporations, economists, and endless others about how good the American economy is, let's consider a few basic points. Are there any facts? Of course there are, but they are being used to mislead rather than lead. For example, when the administration says that new jobs have been added, it doesn't say how many old jobs have been lost in the same period. Nor does it say what kinds of jobs have been "created" and how much they pay, or what kinds of old jobs have been lost and how much they paid. Could there be a reason? Yes! The unfortunate truth is simply that much more has been lost than gained. In addition, the "gain" relative to population growth is assuredly less than desirable on any basis. If these points weren't true, why then would they be afraid to give us the facts?

Facts from the Bureau of Labor Statistics.
Re-training to earn less!

On Sunday, March 27, 1994, the following letter, written by a lady in Pittsburgh named Iris Kaufman and headed "Re-training to Earn Less," appeared in the "Letters to the Editor" section of *The New York Times*.

When politicians and economists speak of re-training people who lose jobs that pay well, whom do they have in mind? According to a Bureau of Labor Statistics list, the occupations that are projected to add the most jobs between 1992 and 2005, assuming moderate economic growth, include: nursing aides, orderlies and attendants; waiters and waitresses; janitors and cleaners; salespeople, cashiers, general office clerks, truck drivers and food preparation workers. The remaining two, registered nurses and computer systems analysts, are the only ones that require education much beyond the eighth grade. Are college instructors, engineers, administrators and out-of-work professionals of all kinds going to be re-trained as service providers? If so, it seems our standard of living won't be headed up for a very long time.*

This letter clearly makes some very good points in its brief message. However, a couple of further thoughts dealing with its basic story are useful.

Certainly such occupations pay low wages for the most part. More important, this country apparently has no plan to provide sufficient jobs that pay well. If it does, the plan has to be the best kept secret since World War II. We have far too few jobs right now for our unskilled, semi-skilled, skilled, and

---

*From the viewpoint of 2010, it is remarkable to see how prescient these views were.

managerial job-losers to fill. Too many companies in this country continue to knock out jobs in the U.S.—"re-engineering," "re-structuring," "down-sizing," "right-sizing," while expanding overseas directly or indirectly ("outsourcing").

And there is no way to regain these jobs in sufficient number until we go back to making things—products for our own market as well as international markets. And what about jobs as our population continues to increase? From where are those jobs going to come? From the heavens? They aren't, anymore than jobs at this very moment do, if this nation doesn't act on what is needed—soon! *This country needs the kinds of jobs that can be filled by the people who have lost their jobs—not jobs beyond their experience, knowledge, or capability.*

Another obvious and absurd situation is the billions of dollars being spent on training for jobs that don't exist. Equally insane is training people whom companies would not hire even if the jobs did exist—the over-fifties; over-qualified people; individuals considered to be wedded to a profession or industry (deemed to be inflexible); high school drop-outs; those judged to have inadequate education; people who have been on government support programs; men and women of checkered backgrounds; long-term homemakers; those highly qualified in a different area ("overqualified" again); and still others of untold categories.

How good can a "strong economy" get?
Not very with Wall Street calling the shots!

The New York Times quoted these Agriculture Department figures for 1994. Federal food assistance programs—presumably meaning people who need help to get food—list school lunch program participants at 25.3 million; participants in the special supplemental nutrition program for women, infants and children at 6.5 million; people receiving food stamps at 27.5 million (soaring from 20 million in 1990, up more than a third). That's an incredible percentage of this nation's population, about one-fifth. Truly a damning commentary!*

In the same issue of this newspaper, the Commerce Department is quoted as stating that the U.S.'s worldwide merchandise trade deficit for 1994 was $166.3 billion, up more than 25 percent from the previous year.** Who's kidding whom? Those billions aren't just dollars. They represent millions of American jobs lost and moved out of this country in one way or another.

That's another reason (beyond automation, which is a legitimate factor) why the United States and many large corporations in this country con-

---

*And it's even worse today. In 2008, there were more than 30 million in the school lunch program; 8.7 million participants in the special supplemental nutrition program for women, infants and children; and more than 30 million people receiving food stamps. As of February 2010, the number of those receiving food stamps had reached 39.68 million.

**These numbers were to get worse and worse. According to the Commerce Department, for all of 2009, the U.S. deficit in goods and services totaled 381 billion—down dramatically from the $696 billion deficit in 2008 and half the record $760 billion gap in 2006. What the far lower figure in 2009 than those in 2006 and 2008 represents is not a country producing more, rather a country buying far less because of the economic cataclysm. The 1994 figure of under a half that of even 2009 reflects the tragic erosion of American jobs in that time. These facts are devastating, bespeaking as they do the ever-growing disaster that we have experienced.

tend that our productivity continues to improve and is the highest in the world again. Why wouldn't that be the case? We continue to sell jobs to other countries that pay slave labor rates while these corporations maintain or increase sales, with far fewer employees and lower costs. It doesn't really require a Ph.D. in mathematics to figure it out!

Unfortunately the "leaders" and "plunderers" don't care what this "productivity rate" means to our country, its people, and their jobs—devastation! Such "productivity" protects the interests of the guilty—their golden parachutes, Swiss bank accounts, etc. And, strangely enough, it's not called sedition or treason! We need to re-think much else regarding what has happened to this once great nation that is now our poor, benighted country—and not just jobs (which, though critical, are only a part of the whole scary picture). Another time, perhaps.

"In the past five years American corporations have eliminated 1.4 million management jobs."

> "Much of the attrition has been due to the re-engineering movement, which *chopped out* whole levels of command, *empowered workers*, *streamlined operations*—and *multiplied profits . . .*
> —Subtitle and quotation
> from an advertisement touting a book
> entitled *Reengineering Management.*

What were once the values of American business are being sordidly sold down the river, and according to this advertisement, that should be a source of pride for us. Wouldn't it be a brighter future if we could claim 1.4 million such jobs had been added because of economic expansion and the resulting increase in opportunities? What a searing contradiction of success! The perversity of making something bad—lost jobs and annihilated families—come out as being good is a little less than noble. In fact, it is plain rotten and clearly unworthy of decent people. And what about non-managerial jobs lost? Guess they don't even count!

Are the "leaders" simply unaware of the realities? No! Most just prefer to feather their own nests and not rock their boats.

Do the "leaders" know that eventually without regaining our manufacturing base and *real* jobs, there will be only limited income even for service people, since there will be little to service (with agriculture and natural resources not being remotely enough) and with foreign countries and companies repatriating their own service functions? And, with only a small fraction of our former total business base in operation, our ability to buy will dwindle? Also, as our ability to buy diminishes (two-thirds of our economy presumably, we are told, being dependent upon consumer buying), our literal survival capability will be compromised. Yes, but too many think that by such time they will have theirs (loot, that is) and be scot-free.

It would appear that among the "leaders" a group believes in the omniscience of a hidden elite; many don't understand the realities; others don't want to hear, much less understand; some simply believe the disintegration will take longer than is of concern to them; another x number has been bought; and for the remainder there might be still unknown reasons. However, regardless of the reason, the danger for America and its people is beyond measure—certainly in terms of *real* jobs and a desirable standard of living. There is also danger for our very survival as a free nation (how do we protect ourselves if we don't make many of our own critical defense needs but import them instead?) and as a unique culture.

Overtures have been made to the power structure on several occasions over the last three administrations (seventeen years) and to several of the major media. These were overtures for understanding of the prospective job devastation and specific action courses to counter the impending problems that subsequently materialized and are now massive messes. The claimants of "the healthiest economy ever" have no concern for, or want no part in, hearing the facts of our dire straits, much less letting anyone else learn about them.

It is worth further mention that the Reagan Administration proclaimed we were in a post-industrial era, a service economy, and a high-tech society. Unfortunately, as pointed out earlier, they had no answers at all to the crucial questions!

(1) With what are you going to replace all the industries lost and being lost?

(2) How long will it take?

(3) Where are you going to get the trillions of dollars necessary for the replacements—if you know what they are, which you admit you don't?

(4) What are you going to do with our millions of "disemployed" people in the interim years—if you know how many people and for how long a time, which you also admit you don't?

At one time during the Reagan Administration it seemed that there night be some hope for understanding and action under Vice President Bush. That hope evaporated after he became the president and was successfully shut off from reality by the Praetorian Guard.

But wasn't the Clinton Administration's cry "It's the economy, stupid!"?
Yes, but not our economy, with jobs for Americans!

The Clinton Administration seemed to offer hope during the campaign. Then the Clinton Labor Department "leadership" decided (but not a young, key staff member who thought differently and did his best with zero success) that American jobs, God forbid, might get in the way of NAFTA (the North American Free Trade Agreement) and GATT (the General Agreement on Tariffs And Trade). So, guess who won? Not Americans! The Council of Economic Advisors was also approached. Same fate! Several senators were sought out during the first half of the Clinton Administration. Despite interest from their major staff people, they were "working on NAFTA" or "too busy" for American jobs to distract them.

It should be noted that all of these "NAFTA-niks" must have worked very hard, but not very well or very effectively, on researching the facts not just about jobs but about the Mexican economy itself! Were this not the case, they would have uncovered the delusions and lies about that economy.

It was these misses among other things that led to the peso meltdown and the economic crisis. Otherwise, wouldn't our "leaders" presumably have informed the American people and changed their position accordingly? The people of this country are going to pay a very high price for the bad Clinton Administration research and the Clinton bailout of Wall Street, Mexican investors, the Mexican Government and American corporations. Despite all claims to the contrary and regardless of the repayment schedule, much was sacrificed.

Where is the union "leadership?"
Concerned with the money
for their re-training programs, not jobs!

It was also determined through an honest but lonely voice in the shrine of the American labor movement that unions wouldn't be interested in courses of action that could produce *real* jobs in manufacturing. They were committed to the Labor Department's job re-training "initiative" for jobs that don't exist.

At the time, it was a 3.5 billion dollar budget, and Labor's "leadership" was seeking 7 billion. Interesting? Appalling! That was the last hope. If the unions aren't interested in *real* jobs for Americans, who is? What is the court of last resort? This book! It was at that juncture the idea for this book was born—out of absolute despair for the plight of American workers, the very life-blood of our country, and for our country itself.

What about the media? Not much good!

In the area of the media, efforts were limited and met with even less success—no responses at all! Yet at various times over the years—from 1980 to 1994—several important national media were approached, including weekly news magazines, major business publications and some of the leading daily newspapers.

Furthermore, the media overall are steadfast in refusing to confront their interviewees or press conference subjects with penetrating questions about jobs. Jobs gained? Jobs lost? What types of jobs in both cases? What has been the average pay of jobs gained? And those lost? What are the specific strategies for developing *real* jobs—not temporary or part-time—in large quantities? No re-training for non-existent jobs baloney! No NAFTA delusions! No double talk! No endless words with no point!

This Administration can talk forever on the subject of jobs and say absolutely nothing—doing it glibly, charmingly and seemingly with total conviction! Unfortunately, total conviction about nothing is nothing. Yet they offer it with consummate artistry and as if nothing were everything—issuing their glowing words directly from the Mount on tablets of stone. They don't even blush. And they get away with it! Worst of all, they do nothing to rectify our plight, and they get away with that, too!

The media owe the American people enough understanding of the problem to ask the key questions. They also are responsible for getting the answers—and not being put off by fancy dancing around the issue, pussy-footing away from the subject, tip-toeing through the tulips as a diversionary tactic, or resorting to the old soft-shoe into the wings.

Finally, where does the financial world fall? The worst of the bad guys! And big business? Not much better!

"Leveraged buyouts" are usually manipulated and controlled by Wall Street and its law firms. They cost jobs in droves, because companies are merged, functions duplicated, and then people are dumped into the street. These "investors" (knowing little, if anything, about the business) now control the company; they sell off operations to pay back the money they borrowed to buy it. And finally they demand improved profits from management to run up the price of the stock so that the "investors" can make more money.

The management knows that the quickest way to profits is to cut the payroll. So, jobs are axed without consideration for the future of the company, much less the people. Management retains juicy jobs, royal perks, unbelievable golden parachutes, and so forth. In fact, downsizing has become management chic, and a management that has perpetuated such a rape, with high short-term profits, creates a great demand for its services. Of all, they have to be the most reprehensible!

Eventually what used to be a strong, dynamic enterprise may well go into dissolution or bankruptcy rebirth (and do it all over again) because of such greed and avarice. Nice business! Sell-offs and lay-offs! Wrecked careers; ruined families! Profits at any cost—our jobs and our lives!

Here's an interesting, humorous, but frightening side note. An old Yale friend told this story. Right after World War II, he and several fellows were sitting around at Yale deciding what to do when they graduated. They had two criteria. Where is the weakest, least astute management sales strategy in the business world? And also, where are the biggest opportunities for profits as a result? Guess what they chose? A Wall Street firm now bears their names. It is one of the prestige investment houses in that home of mammon and travesty of the capitalistic system. Moral? Not good! But nonetheless a tale with an ironic twist of black humor. Unhappily, a vast number of charlatans, and worse, with avarice as their god have climbed on the bandwagon of success (learned how to shuffle "paper" and market these "products") while they reaped (raped) enormous ill-gotten gains at Americans' largely innocent expense.

Are facts about job losses available without being swallowed up in the jungle of statistics and lies? Yes, harsh and highly personal facts!

Have you personally been a victim of unemployment? Are there members of your family who have? Do you know friends who were "downsized"? Are there others who were "re-engineered"? What about "restructured"? Or subjected to a "reduction in force" ("riffed")? How about "merged" into the street? Or simply "dumped"? Maybe "terminated" or "fired"? Isn't there something called "early retirement"? Or a "package"? Did we mention military base shut-downs as well as other "closings and consolidations"? And more? "Layoffs," etcetera, etcetera! What about "right-sized"—for an irony?

Are you, or do you know anyone who is in danger of being subjected to one of these?

If we may reprise a little, for emphasis! Small wonder U.S. "productivity" is the highest in the world! People thrown out of jobs in this country; those jobs moved to foreign countries for "slave" wages; the companies involved continuing to do the same amount of business, or more, here. These companies have fewer people to pay in this country; their foreign job costs are a travesty. And that's what we are told is productivity—the highest in the world. One could consider it laughable—if it weren't so sick and disgraceful!

How many Americans are better off at this time than in earlier times? It is a relatively small group. This is the group that is unimaginably better off, "the plunderers" and their beneficiaries! But there is a second group that numbers in the millions. They are not better off but drastically worse off!

Consider this: Anyone in the first group should help solve this jobs tragedy if he or she has any concern at all for family, friends, country, and—frankly—themselves. What has been gained by them requires the well-being of our nation for its preservation in one way or another. Even should a mountain top in Switzerland or the vaults of the gnomes in Zurich have appeal as a fortress to defend their ill-gotten spoils, neither of these refuges (even with an unnumbered Swiss bank account) can protect such interests without a healthy United States of America, despite the gobbledytalk claims about global financial markets' stabilizing effect. People in this group should help, but for the most part won't—and for the very same reasons that they are part of such a group—plain unadulterated greed. The rest (the second group—the millions upon millions who are the unfortunate victims) *must* solve the problem.

What are a few basic numbers that encapsulate this sorry tale?
Here are the sickening realities!
What follows is based on numbers from the U.S. Department of Labor—Bureau of Labor Statistics.*

- As of the second half of 1994, severe unemployment and disemployment distress was far-reaching and afflicted many more people than the Administration would have us believe if we simply took the more available numbers on face value. We were short about 40 million self-sustaining jobs!
- The work pool had around 130 million people in it. Of this total:
  - 8 million were unemployed
  - 7 million were employed part time (but wanted full-time employment) *or* had given up
  - 25 million didn't earn enough to keep a family of four above the poverty level

So, around 30 percent of the potential work force was in severe difficulty. What an ap-

---

*The numbers provided here refer to the 1990s, when this book was originally written. The tragic fact is that, terrible as these numbers were then, the situation is frighteningly worse today as our nation struggles through the most serious "recession" since the Great Depression.

palling situation for a nation that until recently was the envy of the world and literally was without challenge in terms of good jobs for its people!

- During the 1980s two million U.S. manufacturing jobs were exported to low-wage countries in Asia. Five hundred thousand to Mexico. It would be interesting to know how many of the "bosses" who, because of their greed and lack of desire to find a better answer for our country and its people, made these decisions to sell American jobs to foreign countries also prospered enormously from such unconscionable acts.

- In 1993, good-paying jobs in the United States were being lost at the rate of 3,000 a day and accelerating. Yet there is much government and corporate bragging about an 18 percent productivity increase in the last ten years. Little wonder, when millions of jobs were and are being lost by "outsourcing" to cheap foreign labor; income has been virtually static or worse; and "new jobs" are low-paying service, part-time, temporary, no-benefit jobs. Not too helpful when the country is short 40 million self-sustaining jobs!

- Non-agricultural U.S. worker's real weekly earnings fell from $327 in 1973 to $265 in 1990. Hardly the way to the American Dream!

- The percentage of middle-income families in this country has fallen from 71 percent (1980) to 63 percent (1994), while 56 million Americans live in households below the poverty level. Sound like a third-world nation? It will be, unless the trend is reversed!

- In 1989, one out of four U.S. jobs was part-time. That's bad! In 1994, one out of three was! Worse and going the wrong way! Most such jobs offer no pension benefits and no health insurance. Worse still!

- In 1993, 60 percent of the jobs "created" were in low-paying service functions such as employment in restaurants, bars, health care, and temporary work. As of early 1995, the Clinton Administration claims the "creation" of six million plus jobs, but, then as now, they didn't say how many had been lost. Nor did they give the average pay of jobs lost compared to those "created"! Hardly a strategy for restoring the American standard of living!

Further,

- Thomas C. Gibson, a business writer and consultant, quoted labor analyst Harold Meyerson writing in *LA Weekly*, "Our business and political leaders' response to the globalization of markets has been to turn us into a nation of temps." Unfortunately, an insightful and valid commentary about our "leaders"!

- Bob Herbert, in his column for *The New York Times*, under the heading "Workers, Unite!" wrote: "Even Labor Secretary Robert Reich, in a speech that tried to put the best face on the nation's employment picture, acknowledged that the middle class has become an anxious class, most of whom hold jobs but who are justifiably uneasy about their own standing and fearful for their children's futures." Less than a ringing endorsement of what is being done (or—more to the point—not being done) to provide *real* jobs for Americans!

- In the same article, Bob Herbert went on to say that "if employed members of the middle class are anxious and fearful, what is to be said about the many millions of unemployed, partially employed and temporarily employed men and women who arise each day with little or no awareness of where their family's rent or meal money is to be found?"

There can hardly be any more to say about the problem—Except that it is sickening to realize our great nation has been brought to its knees by its so-called "leaders"as a result of this *real* jobs failure which has occurred in a relatively short time!

Has anybody else put the realities together? Yes, one of the country's most respected economists!

This former dean of a premier management school at a leading university (an individual who wishes to remain nameless for his own sadly good reasons—has a family and can't afford to lose his job!) reached essentially the same figures for the percentage of people in the total work force who are unemployed and underemployed. While he used a different approach to arrive at these figures, his conclusions were basically the same as those presented above: approximately one-third of the work force is looking for work/more work (*real* jobs).

Here is a summary of his breakdown:

WORK FORCE %	PEOPLE IN MILLIONS	CATEGORIES
	7.5–8.0	*Official unemployed*
	5.0–6.0	*Not working* but do not meet tests for work force
	4.5	*Part-time* workers
14%	17–18.5	*Sub-total*
	8.1	Temporary
	2.0	*"On call"*
	8.3	*Self-employed* but not really—down-sized (out of pride, refer to themselves as consultants)
14%	18.4	*Sub-total*
4%	5.8	*Missing* males (25 60 years of age) not in labor statistics, but included in census
32%	41.2–42.7	Total—equals approximately 1/3 of work force looking for work/more work—*real* jobs; without 11 million *immigrants* of illegal standing—a sea of unemployed.

These are author's notes (not the management school dean's):

- Each unemployed person directly affects at least two to four others in a family.
- Unemployed/employed statistics do not cover one person with three or four jobs, one person thus counted as three or four employed.
- Temporary, part-time, "on call" figures do not identify number of "jobs" with no benefits and/or paying minimum wage or less.

CHAPTER 8

IS THERE A SOLUTION TO THIS JOBS DISASTER?
OF COURSE, IF WE GET BEHIND ONE
AND MAKE IT HAPPEN!

How many prospective real jobs solutions are there? Many!

Before considering solutions to this jobs disaster, it should be recalled that what is involved here is a basic economic structural jobs dislocation. It is not what the "leaders" and plunderers would like us to believe. In short, it is in no way a temporary economic cyclical "adjustment" to the erstwhile "new global economy" and the so-called new world market. As mentioned earlier, this country is short more than 40 million self-sustaining *real* jobs and with no place from which they can come under the existing circumstances. Hardly a temporary "adjustment" problem!

What are these solutions?
First, a few key insights.

A short outline for each of some specific possibilities is presented. Undoubtedly there are others. However, let's not confuse temporary measures with real solutions that will last. We also should remember that there may be a need for some interim steps (such as tax and/or interest changes) to make the real solutions quicker and easier. Such steps are not solutions; they are simply ways of facilitating solutions. Also addressed in what follows are issues relating to time, political difficulty, and basic desirability estimates. The bulleted lists of "Advantages" and "Hurdles" are undoubtedly not complete. They are just starter lists containing the most obvious and critical points. (You can probably add many of your own.)

Very different perspectives are the underlying basis for the *real* jobs solutions in the various possibilities covered here. Each of them is offered in a relatively consistent framework so that some comparisons among these possibilities are possible.

The *real* jobs solution *presented first* is an incentives plan that provides substantial money advantage for U.S. companies to manufacture products in this country for domestic consumption (and international markets as appropriate) from parts made here with the assembly work done by U.S. workers. Exceptions would be only for legitimately vital reasons. The incentives plan would also give an immediate and true price advantage to Americans for buying products really made in the United States. Part of the overall incentives plan is a negative incentives penalty in addition to this positive incentives bonus.

The *second solution* is to get one or both major political parties, to develop and implement a *real* jobs plan of their own.

The *third solution* is the creation of a *real* third party, since the two existing ones have had an abjectly dismal record up to this time, as far as providing *real* jobs for Americans is concerned. An absolutely damning record, in fact!

The *fourth solution* is drastic and the worst one of all unless there is no way to get our "leaders" to use another option soon enough. (Even then it is unthinkable unless there simply is no other choice.) This unfortunate solution is a major military campaign or defense build-up (the latter is far less onerous).

A war materiel build-up provides jobs. However, for our own interests, defense and otherwise, those jobs must not be out-sourced (regardless of cost advantage), or the United States will be susceptible to out-and-out blackmail. Outsourcing in this instance would make us infinitely worse off—not only because of more jobs lost but also because it would leave us without the means to defend this nation!

The *fifth solution* again is certainly undesirable unless reason cannot be brought to bear in our "leadership" and a better course of action is found. This solution is a peaceful revolution (in Gandhi's terms, passive resistance). Such resistance is what the Mahatma used in India long ago. His peaceful marches succeeded in getting both the government's attention and action along with world sympathy as well. They also unfortunately caused serious problems for the war effort in Asia during World War II.

There are other possible solutions as well as those already discussed. Most are extreme but, nonetheless, all should be considered as options if some reasonable solution to this basic and critical *real* jobs problem isn't determined and instituted—soon!

1. Can the positive and negative incentives plan for American manufacturers/consumers (explained in chapter 4) be sold in the existing political situation? Nigh on to impossible—but there is an outside chance!

The outside chance of selling this incentives plan depends upon a Congressional majority recognizing the political bonanza to be gained from the combination of positive and negative incentives, or even just the positive incentives alone.

These are some of the ***advantages***:
- Brings back *real* jobs (millions upon millions)
- Brings back substantial individual income to tens of millions of people
- Brings back vast profits (billions and billions) to the United States for the benefit of our own country, not some slave-labor nation (The advantage here is particularly important when such a nation could become a formidable enemy, using profits from the enormous volume of products that it sells us now to build its own military. This advantage could apply to various other plans dependent upon their structure.)
- Brings back tax revenues—personal and business (tremendous total)

Other advantages are:
- Reduces the trade deficit drastically and dramatically
- Reduces national debt rapidly and substantially

Unbelievably, but actually:
- Is self-supporting; in fact, can make an unprecedented profit for the government from large tax revenues

Further, it:
- Affords continuous and long-run solutions —no stop-gap, on-again off-again non-solutions

Also:
- Provides incomes sufficient to support families on a reasonable basis, as used to be true when the American Dream was still alive for most Americans
- With the return of family life, addresses the country's societal problems and its cultural life needs, as well as its economic health

And:
- Works within the existing political situation
- Offers great political strength at the grassroots for a very long time (people remember what brought them back to life!)
- ...Along with many other advantages

Obviously, there are major *hurdles* to be overcome:
- Requires U.S. Government support (Congress and the Administration, if possible)
- Requires union support (volunteered or legislated)
- Requires business/financial community/ industry support (voluntary or involuntary)

There are differences in *difficulty* for the various incentives:

- Support from the three groups mentioned under "hurdles" above would be difficult to get for positive incentives alone.
- Support from the three groups would be extraordinarily difficult to get for the combination of positive and negative incentives.
- Support from the three groups would be virtually impossible for negative incentives alone, i.e., penalties for each job lost to another country and also other unjustified *real* job reductions.
- …Along with other possible difficulties

Today's reality:

The unfortunate truth is that all of the vested interests affected will scream like stuck pigs and use each and every dirty trick in the book, legal and illegal, to thwart any such possibility. Their arguments will masquerade under every known façade of decency and righteousness. The reality, however, will be the exact opposite—no concern whatsoever for this once great country and its real people.

Again, their concerns will be for their own selfish interests and those of the people involved with them in various ways. The concerns will be solely for their own greedy, avaricious purposes! Any exceptions? Of course, but very few. Some such exceptions are those who have honest and sincere but misguided philosophical and economic beliefs. One such belief might be that it is more important to protect 10,000 service jobs related to importing auto parts than have 100,000 jobs making those parts in the United States. Undoubtedly there are other kinds of exceptions.

If their beliefs weren't misguided (whether from cupidity or stupidity), the disastrous trends occurring in this country would not exist, but they do. The tragic evidence is inescapable.

These realities are the result of massive problems in this nation that have been caused by policies and actions springing from nothing less than monumental failures in judgment, be they innocent or otherwise. Unfortunately there probably have been some of both. Starting as far back as World War II, we won a military victory and lost the economic war.

How long would it take to start such an incentives plan? Not long!
Politically difficult? Definitely!
Desirable? Highly!

Positive Incentives—

Estimated Time to Start in a
Major Industry (if implemented).........6–12 months

Political Difficulty....................................Very great!

Desirability......................................Extremely high!

Combined Positive/Negative or
Just Negative Incentives—

Estimated Time to Start in a
Major Industry (if implemented).........6–12 months

Political Difficulty.........................Extremely great!

Desirability......................................Extremely high!

2. Can either major political party be convinced that it should develop and implement its own real jobs program? Not impossible—but the next thing to it!

There are two basic issues involved in this possibility. The first is whether the political will exists to stand up against high-powered forces that lobby both parties strenuously such as importers; forces including corporations that profit from slave labor in other countries; large retailers; foreign countries that export enormous amounts of manufactured goods to the United States (such as Japan, etc.).

The other issue is the question of actual capability to produce such a plan. When the only prospective solutions that party leaders seem to grasp are tax and interest rate manipulations—which clearly are not adequate to the task as they have been used—there have to be serious concerns in this regard. In fact not just concerns, but virtually overwhelming doubts!

As with the incentives plan, the probability here of convincing either party on the merits is very low. Otherwise, one of them would have done the right thing long ago. Nonetheless, there is always hope. If one party or the other could see the inevitable reality of a country that turns its back on both parties unless there is a real solution to the *real* jobs problem soon, then a true possibility would exist. Should either party recognize the opportunity it could gain if it were the one to develop such a program, the possibility would rapidly turn into a probability.

Here are several ***advantages*** such a program must provide (similar to the advantages of the positive/negative incentives):

- Works within existing political situation
- Brings back *real* jobs (millions upon millions)
- Brings back substantial individual income to tens of millions of people
- Brings back vast profits to the United States (billions and billions)
- Brings back tax revenues—personal and business (enormous total)

Also:

- Reduces the trade deficit drastically and dramatically
- Reduces national debt rapidly and substantially

Additionally:

- Affords continuous and long-run solutions
- Provides adequate incomes to support families on a reasonable basis (the American Dream)
- Re-establishes the foundation to address the country's societal problems and restore its cultural base

Lastly:

- Offers virtually limitless political strength at the grassroots level for a very long time. (People remember the sources of jobs! President Roosevelt is still remembered in this respect both by Democrats and

Republicans; in other ways, not always positively)
- …And numerous other advantages

Again there are substantial *hurdles* to be jumped although they are not all parallel to the hurdles associated with the incentives plan:
- Works against myriad lobbies—corporate, GATT, NAFTA (if it still exists), importers, retailers, Wall Street, foreign countries and on and on
- Poses major political risks (if not done right and implemented properly)
- Raises question of either party's capability to do the job
- Requires putting America and its people above personal self-interest of various kinds, not to mention simple greed
- As well as other hurdles

Today's reality:

As discussed above, politicians' (statesmen are few and far between these days!) solutions to economic problems (jobs most importantly) revolve around taxes and interest rates and sometimes retraining or make-work programs.

Such approaches clearly don't succeed in any longer-term sense. At best, they are stop-gaps. At worst, they are a deliberate snare and delusion which proffers false hopes. There is no instance in recent history (except President Roosevelt) that comes to mind which was an exception. It is also true that politicians don't bite the hand that feeds them (lobbyists, pressure groups, vested interests of major individual supporters, etc.). So, this program faces an uphill battle. However, in the final analysis the real question is how many in Congress realize how great is the threat to this country—and themselves as well—posed by the lack of *real* jobs for Americans. Are sufficient numbers of our legislators aware of this? Unlikely! Although the hope should be that there actually are enough real patriots to do the job; so far—unfortunately—the evidence is to the contrary, and as such anything but encouraging.

How long would it take to get such a program?
Probably forever (if even then, given record).
How difficult? Beyond belief!
Desirable? Infinitely.

Estimated Time to Start
(if implemented).................................Years (if ever)

Political Difficulty...........................Extremely great

Desirability.......................................Extremely high

3. A new major political (in a positive sense) force that cares about the country and all the people—a real third party! Possible? Absolutely!
Quick enough for the real jobs crisis? Absolutely not!

A new third party with real consideration and concern for this country's people would be a monumental step forward for the nation—but not for *real* jobs in anything like a reasonable time. Such an endeavor takes a lot of time, particularly at the congressional level. Could a new third-party president create *real* jobs without having strong third party representation in congress? Conceivably yes. However, it would be nothing short of a miracle!

Unfortunately, new third-party efforts in the recent past have probably set such a possibility back by a rather substantial amount. Nevertheless, in the shorter term, any such movement with even limited appeal could have a substantial horsetrading position. Were there such an organization with a *real* jobs mission, its influence in this regard might be felt (in congress, in state and local governments, and in the nation as a whole) long before major political success was achieved.

The assumed (and hoped for) ***advantages*** are:
- Puts the nation first
- Is based on the fact that *real* jobs are essential to the solution of our country's other problems—societal, cultural, economic, international, and so forth
- Allows for openness to ideas, not just vested interests
- Works, it is to be hoped, on the basis of having qualified people—not cronies, good ol' boys, financial backers in positions of responsibility
- …Along with other advantages

Unfortunately, the ***disadvantages*** are formidable:
- Represents an unprecedented development in the nation's history
- Demands charismatic leadership with

integrity, courage, vision, pragmatism, stamina
- Requires great sums of money to win just the presidency, much less lower offices
- Requires a lot of time to find and elect right people at each level
- Necessitates massive organizational efforts
- ...Along with other possible disadvantages

Today's reality:

This possibility is probably the right (and best) solution for the long run. Unfortunately, the nation has to get through its immediate crises in order to get to the longer term. This course of action should undoubtedly be undertaken in the country's future interests. But, because of time and cost, it is not a solution to the jobs trauma, which is the critical need we face right now.

Regardless, a charismatic individual (with the money and the one-time seeming desire of an H. Ross Perot) who is smart, a patriot, and someone who truly cares about the people of this country is absolutely essential for success. This ingredient is vital—no matter what the time factor.

How long for a new party? Long!
How difficult? Difficult!
Desirable? Extremely, but not for real jobs now!

Estimated Time to Start
(if implemented) ....Years (4–10)

Political Difficulty ....Extremely difficult

Desirability..Extremely high

4. Is a major military war (or defense build-up) an option? Quite possibly—although the former is a dreadfully bad one.

A war certainly is something no one with a rational mind could possibly want. However, in some ways there is no worse thing than not being able to feed a family because of joblessness. Witness the reasons many recruits join the armed forces. It's a job even though they know clearly from our recent history that they are deliberately putting themselves into a situation of grave potential danger. There are other reasons, of course, but this has been and is a major one.

As far as a build-up of our defense capability is concerned, there is no doubt that a strong military (all services) is the best possible defense and, unfortunately, the only true deterrent to war at this stage of human history. The worst possible time to reduce the military-industrial complex is when the *real* jobs picture is bleak, as at the present time. Putting people from the armed forces and their industrial support structure into the street when there are no self-sustaining jobs is not just inhumane. It is insane!

We are told that the Cold War is over and therefore our military needs have been greatly reduced. The exact opposite is the case! The world is more unstable now than it has been at any time since Hitler and Stalin. The nuclear arsenal technology of the late Soviet Union is in various and unreliable hands. The tragic fact is that undoubtedly a portion of it is now in the possession of rogue nations and even supposedly respectable nations, with a dire potential for terrorist acquisition.*

Remember, too, that "downsizing" afflicts more than jobs; it operates in the nuclear, biological, and other weapons spheres as well. So, today a suitcase apparently can annihilate a city! Add to all these horrendous dangers the insidious drug warfare that is rapidly consuming the very life force of this nation, and one can make an incontrovertible case for not less but more military strength!

Such military force unquestionably should be redirected and reorganized in various respects—but not reduced. Make it effective—yes! Make it efficient—of course! But don't put our nation on the streets of the world as we find ourselves on the streets of our cities—at risk of our last breath because of a random act of horror! Worse still—a calculated such act!

---

*The dangers we face today as we set out toward the second decade of the twenty-first century are infinitely greater than during the Cold War. Witness the bombing attack on the World Trade Center, the chemical weapons attack in Tokyo, and the disastrous situation in the Balkans. Yugoslavia (Serbia, Croatia, Bosnia) could be just the precursor. Then, consider the possibilities among the previous Eastern Bloc nations; the North Korean travesty; the debacles of Iran, Iraq, and Afghanistan; the terrorist forces (in Syria, Gaza, Yemen, Somalia, Libya, etc.); the Middle East tinder box (the oil reservoir of the world); the African morass; the prospective confrontations between China/Taiwan/Hong Kong; the ongoing tensions between India and Pakistan; myriad terrorist organizations; and on and on. Additionally, some of our "allies" are dubious quantities at best.

A military war (to be avoided at nearly all costs) or defense build-up based in our own country has these *advantages*:

- Puts the nation first
- Forces manufacturing (*real* jobs) back into this country (defense and survival needs)
- Gets the country to realize that *real* jobs are a prerequisite to national life
- Makes recent generations recognize (in a build-up) the essential nature of *real* jobs for all our people but that war is the wrong way to have to get them (however, get them we must)
- Gains the understanding that we must do a better job of fighting economic wars if we are to avoid the horrors of modern, technological military devastation
- Ensures that our corporations know that their allegiance is to this country, not the world, and that their welfare is tied to the welfare of the United States, not some foreign investor or government
- …Along with other advantages

The *disadvantages* (of actual war—not build-up) are beyond words (only the horrors of the actual experience can express the reality)

- Proves the tragic human cost of military warfare
- Provides a belated understanding that failure in economic wars (generally not recognized, much less understood) leads to this horror (there has been a total failure to grasp this even very recent history)

- Evidences the physical devastation that this time would be visited upon our own country in one way or another (frontal attack, terrorists, sabotage, etc);
- Puts the enormous human and financial costs of warfare and its aftermath for the nation (assuming that it and any of the world is left) clearly in view
- Inflicts incalculable harm on all humanity—adversaries and innocents as well
- . . . Along with other untold disadvantages

Today's reality:

This possibility is obviously the worst imaginable way to solve the jobs disaster. We must be smart enough to avoid it at all costs. Our World War II "victory" and our post-war follies—the most directly damaging being the rebuilding of our former enemies' production capability—have incredibly brought us to this sorry jobs plight. The highest price we paid was the loss of competitiveness for our own manufacturing base.

Despite acclaim for the Marshall Plan, and even though there was a critical need for a European buffer against the Soviet Union after World War II, other strategies could have been used. Post-war dangers were real, but the United States was the sole nuclear power of the time. We not only failed to use that leverage, but we had it stolen. However, we should not delude ourselves into believing that we are immune from going to war for the wrong reasons (or the right ones, for that matter) or of making similar devastating mistakes on a future occasion. Unfortunately, there are evil forces at work that would like to have us reach the wrong conclusions and act accordingly. Judicious force, nevertheless, may be necessary in certain unavoidable situations.

A defense build-up for deterrence with the wise leverage or use of power, where necessary to prevent more far-reaching problems, is a different story and a desirable strategy if the real issues, and not politics, prevail in the implementation.

How long? Varies!
How difficult? Quite!
Desirable? No (except for build-up)!

Estimated Time to Start
(if implemented)..........................Substantial (likely two years and up) but dependent upon situation and commitment

Difficulty.....................Very great (re-establishment of manufacturing base)

Desirability ....None (for war) Very high (for build-up)

5. A passive revolution

A passive revolution essentially could be likened to the civil rights marches in the South during the 1960s and the jobs marches on Washington in the 1930s. In essence, a passive revolution is a peaceful demonstration on a major basis for the citizenry to show its disapproval or dissatisfaction with an action, inaction, or policy of government.

Mahatma Gandhi used this weapon in India during World War II. In the process he caused many problems for the war effort (the British in Burma particularly) and in the final analysis had a very major effect (though not what he had sought— the partitioning into India and Pakistan instead of a unified India) upon Indian independence.

Such an approach is not easy, nor is it a quick fix. Nevertheless, it can offer peaceful solutions to serious problems. Therefore, as a tool of leverage in certain situations, it is capable of producing important results and must be a consideration among the various options.

The ***advantages*** of a peaceful revolution (passive resistance) are significant:

- Forces national attention on the jobs disaster
- Can pinpoint culprits who have created or ignored this devastating crisis
- Exerts great pressure to provide a real solution and implement it quickly
- Shows "leaders" and "plunderers" that their days of sacrificing *real* jobs for their personal advantage are at an end
- Demonstrates the force of the people's will.
- ...Along with other advantages

So, too, the ***disadvantages*** are far from incidental:

- Has to have a predetermined jobs plan ready to go
- Takes a lot of time
- Requires extensive organizational efforts
- Demands right, courageous, and charismatic leadership

- Needs substantial financing—but far less than some alternatives
- Must get major media support to augment groundswell effect
- …Along with other possible disadvantages

Today's reality:

This kind of grassroots effort is neither easy nor quick, but it is doable. Once more, as with the new party (third major party) option, the key is charismatic leadership to gain the required momentum and keep up the pressure. Gandhi did it in India, but the form here has to be very different.

How long? Not very!
How difficult? Very!
Degree of desirability? Medium!

Estimated Time to Start
(if implemented) ....Relatively short

Difficulty ....Great

Desirability ....Medium to high

6. Other prospective solutions

This list could probably be endless. Such possibilities as benign dictatorship (not so benign, too, some might say); active revolution (as seen by others); boycotts of various kinds; leverage on U.S. "leadership" in some way so that it drastically and immediately changes its ways (not too likely); and on and on—are all considerations if a solution that actually works isn't operating soon. The people of this country have had enough. They won't put up with it much longer, as well they shouldn't.

How do we start? Rattle the cage now!

GATT or no GATT, NAFTA or no NAFTA, quotas and tariffs and other such measures and worse will be forced down the throats of anyone who stands in the way if this whole jobs travesty isn't fixed—and quickly!

America's "leaders" rape millions of American's jobs! We can stop them. We must!

Call, e-mail, or write the White House, your U.S. senators and representatives soon, and do it repeatedly. Talk to everyone you know, and those you don't, about it! Get action in the media, politics, government, churches, unions, professions, schools, colleges, universities, clubs—any and everywhere you can imagine. All Americans will be hurt badly in due course if this problem continues. It must not. We have to get Americans to understand that America's and Americans' interests and needs come first (most importantly and immediately *real* jobs)—then the rest of the world! (Help other nations, if at all possible, when we succeed in our own jobs solution but not at the expense of American workers' jobs!) Without *real* American jobs America won't be able to help itself much less anybody else!

Get the word out. Word of mouth can start the momentum. Form organizations and spread the word. Start newletters. Do any and everything that will help Americans help Americans.

One of our Presidents once said that the business of America is business. What he missed is that the business of business is our people—employees, customers, suppliers, investors, and so forth. Until rather recently (thirty or so years ago), such was the case and pretty much in this order. No longer!

Now, it's too often just the "plunderers," with their all-consuming greed for money and power, who dictate the interests that are to be served—theirs and theirs only. They are the pariahs and parasites of this world, masquerading under the false colors of democracy, free markets, and the "new global economy." We have to thwart their devastation of our country.

America needs to remember our earlier priorities and force the return to them before it's too late. Too late may come too soon; there's precious little time left before the "real people" will be compelled to take the lead away from the "leaders/plunderers" by one means or another. The "robust economy" and a "record-high stock market" help the wrong people—the people who do not need help instead of the people who do. Helping a small percentage of the nation's people, the greedy, is not helping the large percentage of the nation's people who need *real* jobs.

We must stop the raping of America and millions upon millions of Americans' jobs! America's so-called "leaders" have failed us—disastrously! Facts are facts. Let's do something about them. We must not forget this critical point:

America works when Americans work—in *real* jobs! It doesn't when they don't.

Too many people by far aren't working, and America isn't either!

We must take action now, or our very survival as the nation we have known will too soon be in dire jeopardy.

We can only hope that "too soon" has not already come.

PART THREE
APPENDICES

APPENDIX 1

A Letter to Mr. William Clay Ford

January 9, 2006

Mr. William Clay Ford (the Elder)
Executive Office—World Headquarters
Ford Motor Company
1 American Way
Dearborn, Michigan 48126

Dear Bill,

You probably don't recall our occasional doubles matches at the Little Club back in the days of yore. However, you may remember when Bobby Strasburg and I were summarily drummed out of the Company about 1950 at the end of our training.

We foolishly followed Archie Pearson's desperation suggestion to remove himself from any official responsibility for our innocent, but stupid, good intentions not covered by the rule book.

This appendix was added in 2009.

Archie was our boss in the Ford Field Training Program. He asked us to present "The Missing Link," our attempt at saying thank you to the Company, to Carl Doman at his home. Mr. Doman was then the Vice President in charge of the Service Department. In good faith we did what we were told to do.

The next day Archie had a lapse of memory and denied that he had ever seen our book when asked by Messrs. Bugas and Dunham. We were trainees; he had several kids. We went down—not surprisingly!

Our treatise had been done on our own time in gratitude for all the Program had given us. It used Mr. Doman's department as an example of what we saw to be a critical problem throughout all of the various areas of the Company to which we were given unfettered access during our two years.

In a simple sentence, our report made clear with many hard facts and actual situations that the top management was kept in the dark about what was happening on the plant floor, at the office and in the field. The Service Department, for instance, was losing approximately a hundred million dollars annually through false warranty claims. In those days that was real money, even for Ford Motor Company. Mr. Doman did not appreciate our example, as Archie surmised.

Now that I've gotten in touch with you again after lo these many years, you're probably thinking, well why is he writing to me at this point (maybe he's found a way to speak from the other side of the grass!)? The attached outline will, I hope, explain the reason. It is an attempt to help a Company I've long respected and to save an industry that is vital to this nation's future. The Company's new campaign (newspaper multi-pages) for Ford products is a good move, in my opinion.

Nevertheless, more drastic action is required, as I see it. The American buyer must understand that the once broadly accepted belief about foreign cars being better quality and better value is absolutely no longer the case. Sadly, it has been so for too many years. However, this perception is simply not true any more, based on the information I have been able to glean from sources which are highly reliable in my view.

Anyway, as another attempt at gratitude, this skeletal outline is for a strategic approach to stop the bleeding and counter the foreign incursion of the automobile industry. Admittedly, my knowledge of the Company is from the distant past, but I am confident many strategies have been reviewed in infinite detail, maybe including even the one here. Notwithstanding such a possibility, my guess is that this one has been avoided until the present time and quite rightly for lots of good reasons. However, it seems to me the time has come, and that time is now—if Detroit is going to avert what looks like a desperate future.

Please have a look. If you see merit in the approach, pass it on to your son. My instinct is that he's the kind of young guy who has the vision, brains and guts to turn around this tragic situation confronting Detroit. Remember—back in the late 40's to early 50's the automobile industry was the dynamo of the American economy, accounting for one out of every six jobs in this country directly and indirectly!

The Rouge was the single largest industrial complex on earth. The Big Three owned the U.S. market. Detroit's share was virtually the only share.

Detroit can again be much of what it was—not all, I fear—but still it can recoup in many ways and to a large degree. Detroit *must* once more be the heart of the automotive industry if this poor benighted nation of ours is going to be what it embodied in the American Dream.

Detroit cannot surrender its future to the invasion. Ford's premier legacy has to continue for the United States to prevail in its historical role. The rest of Detroit will emulate Ford in success.

All best,

Peter F. Minnock-Stewart

APPENDIX 2

Detroit—Make or Break!
An Outline

Prospective Solution: Overall Strategic Tracks

1. Take on Japanese, etc., frontally. Otherwise, Ford and GM *are* at grave risk, since appropriate action on the part of the U.S. Government is utterly out of the realm of possibility. Ford *must* fight its own battle for survival and, then, a return to preeminence. Current track is failing. The meaning of "frontally" is covered below.

2. Management of manufacturers *must* create style advantage and ensure quality capability. Also, management compensation must be rational and fair—not 400 to 1 or whatever, as in too many companies (CEO/average worker).

3, Union management *must* do their part—workmanship, labor rates, and total compensation with a reasonable basis.

This appendix was added in 2009.

4, The attack is to be head-on! "We produce *better* cars and small trucks than foreign makers! *You* can prove it to yourself. Use *your* criteria for whatever *you* want" (not the words, just the idea). There probably should be some kind of incentive for proving it to yourself—monetary or otherwise. (Don't know what that should be—needs study.)

Please Note

This outline is essentially reversed, with the prospective solution positioned at the beginning. Why so? Very simply, the reason is to get your attention for the heart of the matter—the basic idea.

At first glance, the approach is a "shocker"! The strategy hits the competition where it hurts most—their strength with buyers. Until recently such an attack has not seemed possible given what is understood to be the heretofore unfortunate realities.

5. The challenge would be along these lines—again not the words. However, the focus should be emphasized as when Ford used "Quality is Job One." Japanese makers should always be mentioned in headline of advertisements and lead-in of commercials!

For example (not copy, just thoughts!):

"Quality Is What We Make—Compare Toyota or Honda"

"Quality Is All We Make—Compare Toyota or Any Other"

"Quality Is What Counts—On All Counts" (engine, transmission, panel fit, amenities, styling, etc.)."

Compare against Toyota, Honda, or any Other"

"Our Quality Is Higher (than Toyota, Honda, and—if you disagree after comparing—we'll . . ."

"Our Cars' Quality Measures Up on All Counts. Test Them on Whatever Counts with You—against Toyota, Honda or Any Other"

"Our Cars' Quality Matches or Beats Toyota, Honda, etc. on Whatever Counts for You! Prove It to Yourself."

The Crux!

I. THE SITUATION

A. GOVERNMENT ACTION—DESIRED

An equalization formula* for U.S. tariffs to account for pollution controls, pensions, health care, other benefits, labor rate differentials, child labor, slave labor, prison labor, subsidies and so forth that put U.S. automotive manufacturers at a severe disadvantage with foreign makers.

B. GOVERNMENT ACTION—ABSENCE

The administration and Congress will do nothing to equalize the U.S. market for domestic automotive manufacturers versus foreign manufacturers' vehicles. They are the true embodiment of "do-nothing" politicians. Hence plant closings,

---

*For Equalization Formula description, please see addendum on page 191.

job losses, infrastructure devastation and serious jeopardy for what not so long ago was the dynamo of the American economy are consuming Detroit on the funeral pyre of political expediency and globalization greed. We should not be misled by the building of foreign makers' plants in the U.S. They are the result of a shrewd, calculated strategy to counter any real U.S. Government action were such an eventuality ever to occur. Their claim would be American operations, American workers, American suppliers. But even under such a guise, the profits still go home.

C. MANAGEMENT FAILURES— MANUFACTURERS AND UNIONS

Both U.S. management groups have failed dismally in reaching workable solutions.

D. EQUALIZATION FORMULA

Even were such a possibility—equalization formula—in the cards, which it isn't, U.S. manufacturers and unions should be required to compete on a *fair* basis—with consumers free to choose any make (domestic or import) on basis of quality, style, price, etc.—or fail.

E. CONSUMER ORIENTATION

By far the world's single largest consumer market, U.S. consumers in general (not all—but a vast majority) have been educated to believe that cheaper is smart in any product category, and too often cheapest is best. For automobiles, witness rebates, no interest loans, leasing deals and so on. However, in the case of cars and small trucks, quality, styling and repair (durability—repair frequency, parts cost, repair simplicity and more) are major purchase considerations (anecdotal; not empirical projectability). Nevertheless, such assumptions seem to be reasonable possibilities if the past is any indication.

Unfortunately, consumers do not grasp the ultimate effect of buying foreign vehicles, any more than they grasp the ultimate effect of shopping at Wal-Mart or supporting Chinese low-price products in general; loss of jobs, reduction of purchasing power until loss of manufacturing and service businesses will lead to no money to buy anything, regardless of its origin. Still, they generally believe cheaper is smarter.

U.S. provides technology that other nations replicate— e.g., China's greater technology exports than U.S. for the first time. In this regard, witness also China's knock-off of virtually any and everything, U.S. patents notwithstanding. They are simply ignored. Even worse, the U.S. trade deficit with China builds China's military to be potential enemy ultimately.

Remember, too, that Japan's automotive technology came from Detroit in 1940's and 50's. It was acquired by hordes of Japanese each with a non-stop camera, granted free access to all production facilities, "Don't worry; they just make that plastic junk." So they did then. And now? Some with WWII experience knew better. They knew that the Japanese had a long vision; persevered; and were clever. Such warnings unfortunately were cries in the wilderness and completely ignored, cast off with self-serving comments that have been self-immobilization for Detroit.

II. THE PROBLEM

Prospective loss of critical U.S. industry accounting for
millions of jobs and tax revenues.*

III. PROSPECTIVE SOLUTION

A. OBJECTIVES

   1. Quality

   2. Styling

   3. Overall

B. QUALITY—STRATEGY

From what I hear, (admittedly anecdotal). U.S. manufacturers'
quality is at least very close to, if not equal to, that of
Japanese and other foreign makers. Use it!

C. STYLING—STRATEGY

Lags but is gaining and promises substantial improvement.
Take lead from Mustang, Corvette, Chrysler or earlier
Italian designers. Adapt and capitalize on them! Be
distinctive. Have character for each line. Separate from
pack. Then find another Harley Earl. (All personal
opinion.)

---

*Don't know actual numbers anymore, but they have to be daunting!

ADDENDUM

The equalization formula amount for each unfair cost advantage such as anti-pollution controls, and all the others, should apply not only to imports but also to every foreign unit sold in the U.S. regardless of the country where it was assembled—be it the country of origin* (including the possibility of an even lower cost alternate source) or the U.S. Only by such a provision can so manifestly calculated a stratagem of assembly plants being built in the U.S. (profits going back to the nation of the manufacturer in any event) be blunted and the domestic industry be put on an equal footing.

In like manner, U.S. manufacturers should face the same equalization for all components, sub-assemblies, and final vehicles produced outside the U.S. for sale or use in the U.S. In this way alone (a true equalization formula for all production outside of the U.S. intended for sale or use in the U.S.) can the U.S. manufacturing infrastructure and U.S. jobs be restored on a *fair* market basis.

There obviously are many ramifications, given the complexity of automotive manufacturing, for any equalization formula. However, they can and should be handled individually as the need arises if such equalization is to be a realistic possibility. With the political implications involved, probability theory doesn't afford even modest hopes, much less actual expectations, for legislation that would enact an equalization formula of this nature or any other for that matter.

_____

*Note that certain countries of origin have greater unfair advantages than others. The present situation will worsen with China's entry.

Maybe someday equalization for a *fair* market will materialize when this nation comes to its senses and realizes that otherwise the next stop is the American dump, *not* the American Dream! In the interim, Detroit must fend for itself and win back its market share by beating the interlopers at their own game.